TAKE COMMAND!

THE MODIFIED MILITARY PLANNING PROCESS TO
DISCOVER YOURSELF, UNCOVER WHAT DRIVES YOU
AND TAKE OWNERSHIP OF YOUR LIFE

K.M. HUNTER

Take Command! © 2021 by K.M. Hunter. All rights reserved.
Published by Author Academy Elite

PO Box 43, Powell, OH 43065

www.AuthorAcademyElite.com

All rights reserved. This book contains material protected under international and federal copyright laws and treaties. Any unauthorised reprint or use of this material is prohibited. No part of this book may be reproduced or transmitted in any form or by any means, electronic or mechanical, including photocopying, recording, or by any information storage and retrieval system, without express written permission from the author.

Identifiers:

LCCN: 2021918024

ISBN: 978-1-64746-892-7 (paperback)
ISBN: 978-1-64746-893-4 (hardback)
ISBN: 978-1-64746-894-1 (ebook)

Available in paperback, hardback, and e-book.

Any Internet addresses printed in this book are offered as a resource. They are not intended in any way to be or imply an endorsement by Author Academy Elite, nor does Author Academy Elite vouch for the content of these sites and numbers for the life of this book.

For Bryson.

CONTENTS

Author's Preface x

INTRODUCTION

Chapter 1 - Military planning modified to plan your life . 2

    Understanding what is really important 4

    Keeping sight of the bigger picture. 5

    The importance of the little things we do each day . . . 7

    How this book works. 9

PART I: TAKE STOCK

Chapter 2 - Step 1: Discover yourself. 14

    Writing your Life Map – Phase 0 20

    Example Life Map – Phase 0 22

    The past is a predictor of the future 26

    Not quite finished with Step 1 just yet... 28

Chapter 3 - Step 1: Discover yourself – Tools. 30

    Personality testing 31

    Cognitive dissonance. 33

    Self-esteem vs self-efficacy 35

    Self-discrepancy theory 38

    Step 1 Summary 40

Chapter 4 - Step 2: Uncover what drives you 42

    Vulnerability and Capability Statements. 43

    Life Philosophy. 46

    Life Drivers. 50

    Step 2 Summary 57

Chapter 5 - Step 3: Uncover your world. 58

    Stakeholder domain -
    I'll have what he's having 60

    Physical domain -
    The ocean makes me feel alive! 66

    Information domain -
    I saw it on the internet, so it must be true 70

    Step 3 Summary 74

PART II: TAKE CONTROL

Chapter 6 - Step 4: Design your Life Map 78

    Where to from here? 80

    Milestones and goals 81

    Timeline design. 84

    Where are your Life Drivers? 89

    Life Map example 91

    Step 4 Summary 94

Chapter 7 - Step 5: Enhance your Life Map 96

    What is Life-gaming? 99

    Risk Assessment. 100

    Divergent Points 102

Life-game examples 104

Step 5 Summary 111

PART III: TAKE COMMAND

Chapter 8 - Step 6: Take Command. 114

Implement routines and habits. 115

Remember your Life Drivers and your Life Philosophy 115

Review and update 118

'Step 7': The Black Swan event. 120

Step 6 Summary 122

Chapter 9 - Conclusion. 124

Appendix 1 126

Appendix 2 130

Appendix 3 134

Appendix 4 135

Appendix 5 137

Appendix 6 138

Reference Material 140

Acknowledgements 142

AUTHOR'S PREFACE

There I was, little five-year-old me, ready for my first school athletics carnival. I was an energetic child who was not lacking in confidence. There were three races for my age group; the first was a sprint that I won easily. At the presentation after the race, I stood up to receive my reward and watched as the other little girls were awarded a green ribbon for third place and a red ribbon for second place. I waited excitedly to see what colour mine would be. When a blue ribbon for first place was pinned to my chest – I was not happy! I did not want a blue ribbon; I wanted a pink ribbon. Pink was my favourite colour. I wondered why, if I had won the race, I did not get to choose what colour ribbon I received. What was the point of winning if you did not want the prize?

After winning the first race and learning the process, I went on and won the backwards running race and was awarded another blue ribbon. It was at this point I decided that if I could not have a pink ribbon then I wanted a red one. I did not want another blue one. I went into the sack-jumping race, determined to come second and achieve my new goal of obtaining a red ribbon rather than just trying to win.

Believe it or not, deliberately coming second was a huge challenge. Trying to win first place is simple, you just run as fast as you can. To come second requires strategy. I started the race jumping along as fast as I could, so I was coming first, then as I got closer to the finish line I slowed down and checked my flanks. I looked to the right and to the left, trying to ascertain who was coming in second behind me so I could let them pass me. It was almost impossible to tell. All the other little girls were almost in a perfect line and identifying who was coming second was difficult. My heart raced with adrenaline as I slowed my pace, frantically looking left and right to make sure I timed it perfectly to come second, scared that a slight miscalculation could see me come in first – or even worse, third! As we bounced over the finish line, I held my breath in anticipation, waiting for the announcement…Coming deliberately second required so much more effort, stress and strategy… But I did it! I had managed to come second!

Winning that red ribbon was the hardest race for me that day. But I had pulled it off, and I was so proud of myself.

I have recalled this amusing story over the years, surmising that I was not particularly competitive. However, on contemplation I realised rather than not being competitive, it demonstrated just how competitive I could be – just not always according to other people's expectations. Usually for me it was about competing against myself. I knew I had always put pressure on myself to achieve my goals, but it was 30 years after that sports day when I truly realised that, for me, the race was never really about other people. It was about competing with my own expectations.

For many years I have written annual or short-term goal lists; things I wanted to achieve in the next week, month or year. I have also had long-term goals or aspirations sitting in the back of my mind, waiting for the opportunity to be acted on. Despite this, I often felt like I did not have a great deal of control over where my life was heading. Being in the military on a two-yearly posting cycle, sometimes less, with deployment opportunities taking me overseas for six or seven months at a time, planning more than one year ahead did not seem practical. However, I eventually realised that my short-term goal setting was not helping me create the life I really wanted.

I had set goals and written to-do lists extensively since I was a teenager and had achieved a great deal due to my goal setting. Yet I was constantly feeling lost and restless, with no idea where my life's journey was really taking me. And despite being a 'take action' type of person, I still felt there was so much of my life where I was waiting for things to happen, or waiting for external circumstances to be right, before I could move in a certain direction. Being a professional analyst and planner, it was natural for me to draw on this knowledge and experience to develop a method for my own Life Plan. By adapting the Military Appreciation Process, and incorporating principles and concepts from risk assessment, philosophy and psychology, I developed a thorough and practical life planning process. The process is scalable, and you can incorporate as much or as little into your own planning and goal setting as you like. You can also apply this process to making major life decisions and transitions, when you are facing something and are not sure what you should do. Using this process, you can take command and live the life you desire.

Author's Preface

I come to you as a fellow student of life who simply wants to share what I have learned from creating and acting on this life planning process. I do not profess to have all of the answers, and my own Life Plan is an ongoing project. It has helped me gain clarity, to understand myself and decide what I truly want out of my life. This is the reason I want to share it with you. I want to show you how you can Take Command of your life journey; to make decisions that will enhance your life and act on them with confidence.

This book aims to provide you with analytical techniques to facilitate self-assessment to understand what drives you and where dissonance exists between the life you have and the one you want to be living. It will give you the tools to build a structured Life Plan, which has been modelled from proven military planning methods. Whatever age you are right now, it is never too early or too late to start filling your life with what you want and stop wasting time on the things you do not want. It is important to not be afraid of planning for the unknown or unexpected. This is what military planning teaches us, to plan effectively in the fog of war where uncertainty and danger are constant companions. It is possible to create a Life Plan even when you do not know exactly what life is going to throw at you.

So, are you in a race, running aimlessly and without a strategy, towards a finish line with no idea what the reward is? Or are you trying to win a race for a prize you do not want, like me as a five-year-old? If so, do not be afraid to change the goal so you can get your sought-after red ribbon, even if it means losing by other people's standards… Or, if you realise you do not actually want any of the ribbons on offer, it is time to get out of the race and go get yourself a pink ribbon. It is time to Take Command of your own life journey.

INTRODUCTION

CHAPTER 1
MILITARY PLANNING MODIFIED TO PLAN YOUR LIFE

> *Plans are of little importance, but planning is essential.*
> —Winston Churchill, former British Prime Minister

'NO PLAN SURVIVES first contact with the enemy' is a common military saying, yet planning is the backbone of every military mission, operation and campaign. Why is this so? Because, although no plan is a guarantee of success, it is through the planning process that you create not just a way to move forward, but a depth of understanding that allows you to make swift, informed decisions when the unexpected happens. The quote by Winston Churchill goes directly to the heart of this concept – effective planning helps prepare you for whatever life throws at you – both the obstacles and the opportunities. It is not the plan that matters so much as the process as you step through to create the plan, and what you learn from it.

The foundation of military planning is the Military Appreciation Process (MAP), a systematic decision-making process that allows the development of logical war-gamed courses of action. There are different versions of the MAP, suitable for different sizes and types of operations. Although each version differs slightly, the key foundational concepts remain intact. A key facet of any MAP is that it is enemy-centric – you must understand the threat to be able to develop a plan that will defeat the enemy. So, you might wonder, how can this be applied to an individual's life? Unless you have a nemesis that you are seeking to defeat, using a military planning process to write a Life Plan seems... well, a bit excessive! But, bear with me.

To transform the MAP into a useful life-planning tool, I have removed the 'enemy' element (Step 3, Threat Analysis) and increased the focus on 'own forces'. In a military context, the Own Forces Analysis examines the size, composition and assets of the military forces assigned to you for your mission. In my modified version, this analysis is looking at yourself – conducting self-analysis of who you are and how your past has shaped you. The first step of the MAP – Mission Analysis – includes Own Forces Analysis. In the modified planning process, I have made Own Forces Analysis a separate component; it is Step 1 in my modified version.

You can see how I have modified the MAP in the diagram below. On the left is the version of the MAP used for individual military planning; on the right, my modified approach (using the same military terminology for the steps).

Military Appreciation Process	Modified Military Appreciation Process
1. Mission Analysis	1. Own Forces Analysis
2. Battlespace Analysis	2. Mission Analysis
3. Threat Analysis	3. Battlespace Analysis
4. Course of Action Development	4. Course of Action Development
5. Course of Action Analysis	5. Course of Action Analysis
6. Decision & Execution	6. Decision & Execution

I have also changed the heading of each step to remove the military terminology and make it accessible for everyone, as you will see when I outline the Take Command Life Planning process below. However, we retain a total of six steps and maintain the integrity of the process flow that will lead you on a journey culminating in a strong, adaptable Life Plan.

Before I outline the Take Command process, I want first to explore the why – why bother spending time developing a Life Plan? What do you gain? I expect that if you are reading this book, you already know the value of writing a Life Plan, or are at least seeking some tools and strategies to improve your decision-making, planning and goal setting. Let us take a moment to consider the benefits of actually following this process and writing a Life Plan.

Understanding what is really important

Going through a life planning process is, first and foremost, a process of self-discovery. In the same way that detailed military planning provides you with an in-depth understanding of your own forces, enemy forces and the battlespace so that you can make quick and effective decisions in the midst of battle, so too, going through a life planning process gives you an in-depth understanding of yourself, your intrinsic motivations and your world. This knowledge then equips you to make confident decisions as you are now armed with a strong understanding of your life goals and what is really important to you. It puts you in charge; you can identify, focus on and work towards your goals, and it gives you the strength to turn down those opportunities that will not make you truly happy.

For example, you may be presented with a career opportunity that appears to be a step forward, something that you want, once wanted, or have been conditioned to want. However, the increase in status and income may involve relocation, or increased travel time or work-hours. Perhaps the opportunity is perfect for you – you thrive in a high-tempo environment, and the time is right to expand on your ambition. But perhaps, by creating a Life Plan, you have identified that you are at a point in your life where your priority is your family, or achieving greater work–life balance. In this instance, additional money and status are not actually going to make you happier; in fact, they could jeopardise your happiness. Having a Life Plan keeps you grounded, allowing you to approach decisions with an objectivity and confidence that will ensure you are not deceived by well-dressed opportunities that actually do not allow you to lead the sort of life that makes you happy.

Keeping sight of the bigger picture

Having a Life Plan allows you to look beyond your immediate, short-term struggles and circumstances to see the bigger picture. It will not stop things going wrong, but it provides context, and shifts your perspective.

Overcoming life's obstacles can be a challenge. Whether it is a physical or mental health challenge, financial struggle, or career or relationship issue, it is very easy to be weighed down in the moment and not be able to see beyond your current difficult circumstances. When you are neck deep in a bad situation, being able to shift perspective and understand that 'this too, shall pass' can give you the breathing space to navigate through the rough patch with greater resilience.

Not long after developing the first version of my Life Map, I moved to a new city to take up a new posting. As a temporary measure, I was living in an apartment, planning to buy a house. A few weeks later, a major natural disaster occurred in north Queensland; my former home, which was 1400 km away, was flooded. The scale of the disaster meant it took almost nine months for resolution of the insurance claim. Throughout this waiting period, I lived with the financial uncertainty and stress of attempting to repair the house while being geographically distant. This event forced me to re-evaluate my plan almost as soon as I had finished it.

Despite the fact that this was not something I had planned for, and that I had prepared for the unexpected by having insurance, I was still in a place where my immediate and even long-term plans were thrown into disarray. Once I assessed my situation and realised it was going to be a long road to resolution, I took a step back and found a way to cope with the situation. Rather than just hoping insurance would cover the repairs and lost income, I adopted a Stoic philosophical perspective. Stoicism is an Ancient Greek philosophy that espouses negative visualisation – you imagine the worst-case scenario to a future event. Negative visualisation mentally prepares you for the worst possible outcome, so that any outcome better than that which you imagined will be welcome. By adopting this perspective, and accepting that the worst-case scenario could occur, I enhanced my resilience. If I had been overly optimistic about the outcome, anticipating insurance would be paid in full, then I would have been financially and emotionally unprepared when this was not the case. I also contemplated how much worse the situation could have been, to remind myself that, in many ways, I was luckier than many other people, and I needed to be grateful for what I did have.

I still hoped insurance would cover the damage, but until a determination was reached, I set my mind to the position that this would cost me tens of thousands of dollars. This meant I needed to stay put in my temporary accommodation much longer than I had anticipated, and to reconsider my financial situation. Rather than letting this event overwhelm me, I was able to focus on a longer-term perspective and realise that I would get through it eventually. Although it meant I had to delay other plans, in the scheme of my entire life this was just something I needed to work through one step at a time.

This event completely disrupted my newly devised Life Plan, but I was equipped to deal with it and manage my expectations. By keeping my long-term goals in perspective, and being flexible enough to adjust my timeline without giving up on my plan, this obstacle proved to be a minor setback in the long run. Just nine months after the flood, I was back on track and ready to keep moving forward, having learnt a great deal and built my resilience in the process.

The importance of the little things we do each day

A Life Plan can not only help you focus on the bigger picture, to look past temporary problems we may be immersed in, it can also provide an opportunity to create healthy and productive daily routines and habits. We all know people who have grand ideas but never follow through. What they have is the goal, or the concept, of what they want to achieve. What they lack is the routine implementation of action that will lead them to their goal. It is no good having a picture of a Ferrari on a vision board and expecting one to magically appear in your driveway one day.

If part of your Life Plan is to own a home within the next five years, you will need to determine the path to get you there. This will require saving money regularly, and maybe a change in certain routines, such as buying only one coffee each work day instead of two. This is the same with maintaining a healthy weight, being fit, spending time on activities you enjoy and being with people you love – by making time in your daily/weekly/monthly routine to focus on the aspects of your Life Plan that will sustain your happiness, you will gain the life you want. In the end, life is made up of the little events that fill each day, so if you are not filling each day with the right things, you will not live the life that you want.

Having a solid routine is the best way to succeed at any aspect of life. Once you have built your Life Plan, it can help maintain the motivation you need to persist in the positive habits that will create the life you want to live. A Life Plan is not just about reaching a future state of happiness or a particular goal, it is about knowing what is important to you, and how you want your life to be, so that you can start living that way now. A Life Plan is not about a destination, it is about the journey.

Having a Life Plan ultimately gives you a life of purpose, meaning and gratitude. It puts you in command of your life, which is how it should be.

How this book works

Take Command outlines a step-by-step planning process organised so that one step flows into the next. Structured in three parts – Take Stock, Take Control and Take Command – the process will unfold into the six steps. Note that the military terminology from the previous diagram has been replaced with new headings that more accurately reflect how the life planning process works for you.

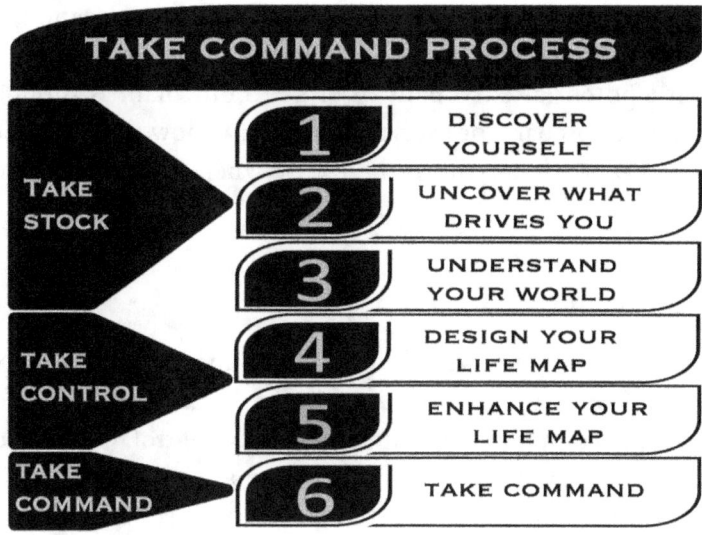

Take Stock

Here we are taking stock of ourselves and our lives. The focus is on examining the journey that has brought you to where you are in your life today, and to assess who you are, what motivates you, and what is most important to you in your world. Here we are conducting self-analysis, analysing our enduring motivations to uncover what is most important to us, and assessing our environment. Before we can move forward, it is essential that we take stock of our journey thus far and appreciate where we are in the present.

Take Control

Here we take control of where our life is heading. Being in control gives someone the power to influence or direct actions or shape the course of events. This part is the nuts and bolts of the planning itself, the 'how', where we develop the course of action that we will take to live our life, to march to the beat of our own drum. An essential part of this is 'war-gaming', or for this process, known as Life-gaming – testing our plan against potential curveballs or risks to our plan. Although you cannot prepare for everything, learning how to Life-game effectively can help you in the future when Fate throws you the unexpected.

Take Command

Here we take command of our life. Command is different to control. Command consists of authority, decision making and leadership; command is executed by having control. Command is often referred to as an art rather than a science, as there is an element of intuition involved; you cannot simply follow a checklist. For this life-planning process, Take Command is the step where you realise the full extent of your authority over the life you live, and you exercise that command in your own way, knowing that the plan you have designed has equipped you to achieve the life you desire.

Before you start, be aware that this is not just a book for reading. To get the most out of this book you need to actually **do** the activities; this will take time. You may prefer to read the book in its entirety and then come back and complete the activities, or you may do them as you go. Either way, the time spent reading this book will likely be a whole lot less than the time you spend working through the activities and writing your plan.

A final word of advice – do not feel that you have to do everything perfectly. Do an activity and move right along. As you will see, the whole concept of a Life Plan is that it is never set in stone; it is always open to change. This is a journey of discovery, and it is ongoing. I cannot advise you how long any of the activities will take, as this varies widely from person to person. But if you take the time to do them wholeheartedly and honestly, you will learn more about yourself and develop a Life Map that will help you on your life's journey. Good luck and enjoy!

PART I
TAKE STOCK

CHAPTER 2
STEP 1: DISCOVER YOURSELF

> *It's called wayfinding, Princess. It's not just sails and knots, it's seeing where you're going in your mind. Knowing where you are by knowing where you've been.*
> —Maui from Disney's *Moana*

WHEN YOU ARE on a journey, you need to stop every now and then and take stock of how it is progressing. There are three things you need to know: where you are now, how you got here, and where you are going. This forms a map by which you can assess your progress, look around and appreciate exactly where you are, before you can determine which path you need to take to continue to your preferred destination.

Because your life's journey started well before you picked up this book, before you start planning where you are going, you

Step 1: Discover Yourself

need to first understand where you are now, and how you got here. To do this, you need to analyse yourself, objectively review your current situation, and reflect on the path that you followed to get here. Armed with that information, you can understand who you are and what you are capable of. This aspect is so essential that the three steps that make up Part I: Take Stock are all focused on analysis of you and the world around you. These need to be completed before planning for the future, which is covered in Part II: Take Control.

Before you look to your past, take a moment to do Activity 1, which will provide a snapshot of where you are now.

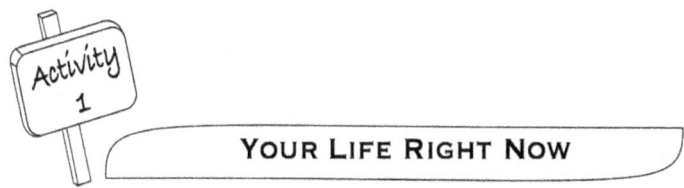

Activity 1: Your Life Right Now

1. Where are you living?

2. Who are you living with?

3. What do you do for work, caring for others, study, volunteering, hobbies etc.?

4. What is your financial situation?

5. How are you living your life? (Include routines and habits.)

6. Who is important in your life?

7. What else is in your life that is important to you?

8. What makes you feel happy and content?

9. What frustrates, angers, scares, or depresses you?

10. Are you living the life you want? Why or why not?

We will not dwell on your current situation any further for the moment; this is a very quick overview of where you are now, to start you thinking as we prepare to look back at the path behind us. You will take a deeper look at your current situation after we take some time to contemplate your past. This is essentially beginning your Life Map – you review your past to understand yourself, and how past decisions (positive and negative) have brought you to this point. As well as being an essential step to planning your future, there are other benefits to this process.

Steiner, Pillemer and Thomsen found that writing about events in your life can increase self-esteem and support construction of positive identity – regardless of the emotional tone and content of the memory. It is easy to see how reliving joyful and successful memories will improve your sense of self, but even writing about negative past events can boost self-esteem. Revisiting the past offers the chance of release, as you are no longer immersed in the stress of the moment. From a distance you can appreciate that your messy divorce led you into a new and better relationship, or that going through cancer treatment changed your outlook on life for the better, and actually increased your happiness.

One way we create a sense of self is by having a life narrative. Your memory, specifically your autobiographical memory, serves to build continuity from the past to the present; this helps form how you see yourself. Autobiographical memory is created through your memories of personal experiences and knowledge about yourself (e.g., where you went to school, where you have lived and worked, and your relationships). It incorporates statements and beliefs about yourself, supported by images or knowledge of past experiences, to form a coherent and enduring internal narrative or understanding about who you are, and the life you have lived. You do not view your life in single event blocks; there is continuity from one event to another – the choices and decisions you make are framed within this narrative. Your past experiences influence your current decisions to shape your future.

Take someone who identifies with being responsible – perhaps they were the responsible sibling, and similar behaviours repeated throughout childhood were reinforced by parents and teachers constantly calling them the 'responsible one'. This child, as a teenager, when faced with opportunities to take illegal drugs, smoke cigarettes or drink alcohol, may have chosen not to, driven by a desire to retain their identity as 'responsible'. Alternatively, they may choose to reject the burden of their 'responsible' identity and decide to be reckless for a change. Depending on which direction they choose, this could be a critical Divergent Point – essentially a fork in the road of their life – with the decision they make having far-reaching consequences that change their life narrative and self-perception.

A good example of this concept can be seen in the movie *The Butterfly Effect*. The main character, Evan, discovers the ability to travel back in time to his childhood and alter life events, but doing so changes the lives of everyone around him. In one reality, his childhood friend is sexually abused by her father, which puts her, in adulthood, in a spiral of destruction; she sees herself as worthless and commits suicide. However, in a different reality, free from abuse, she grows up with healthy self-esteem and is a successful and popular college student. Her brother, in one reality, grows to be violent, dysfunctional and a criminal; however, in another, he is a religious, upstanding young man who, after saving the lives of a woman and infant when he was a child himself, is considered a hero. In each reality, the characters form different autobiographical memories which impact their sense of self and identity, regardless of their enduring personality traits. These drive them to make different decisions throughout their lives in the various realities; these decisions shape their destinies.

In the real world, the significance of autobiographical memory can be observed in people suffering dementia. Their personality can change as their memory deteriorates, and family and friends might feel as they life-game now behave like a different person to who they used to be. As they lose their memory, and with it their autobiographical memory, they start to lose their previously defining traits and identity.

From this, we can see how taking time to write your life narrative can strengthen or even alter your sense of self. The way you choose to look back over your life can help you see what has shaped you – for better or worse. Writing about your life also can distance you from your past, which can help in reprocessing negative events. By understanding the impact of your autobiographical memory on who you are, you can re-write your perspective on your history. Instead of judging yourself, or others, negatively, you can re-write the narrative, which can improve your sense of self, increase self-esteem and enable you to take greater control over your destiny.

Let's consider some examples. When looking back on perceived bad decisions you might have made as an 18-year-old, you have several choices. You can choose to view yourself with a lens of compassion towards your youth and naivety, or continue to be critical and curse your younger self with being stupid, useless or any other negative adjective. Perhaps you may have hated your father for divorcing your mother, but in reviewing your past with a different lens, you might be able to see the situation more objectively and forgive him. Or, instead of feeling

Step 1: Discover yourself

like a victim, you can view your past from a different angle to re-write your narrative as a survivor. Although you cannot change the past, you can change the lens through which you view it. This can be powerful in a way that impacts your sense of self, of who you are, both now and in the future.

This next activity may take some time. It is likely you will come back to this step repeatedly as you start to learn more, or you wish to discover more about yourself. For some people, thinking about their past is not something enjoyable and they will try to skip this part.

If this is you, I urge you to still step through this process, even if you do not go into significant description or recollection. Keep in mind that having sufficient detail from this step will help you develop the understanding needed to uncover your key drivers and develop your plan. On the other hand, the past should be a place of reflection, not somewhere to take up residence. Spending too much time lingering in the past, especially if it involves rumination, can be detrimental. Rumination is repetitively thinking about negative emotional experiences in an overly self-critical way. This differs from simply reflecting on and accepting bad experiences, or contemplating possible solutions and moving forward in your thoughts. The goal of writing about your past is to learn lessons from it; to understand yourself so that you can enhance your present life and set the path in the direction you want your future to be. Knowing where you have come from will help you to understand yourself and to steer your life course in the direction you want to go.

A word of caution: if this part of the process becomes overwhelming due past trauma, consider if you need to stop and contact a professional support or counselling service.

Writing your Life Map – Phase 0

From a military perspective, Phase 0 is what happens before commencement of a declared operation. This phase is generally known as 'shaping' operations as we are shaping the battlespace for possible future operational action. Before looking ahead and building your Life Plan, we need to identify how your past has shaped you into the person you are now, and assess what conditions have already been set to place you in your current position. Thus, Phase 0 is what we will call your life from birth up until this point.

For your Life Map, within Phase 0 you will have several sub-phases: Phase 0a, 0b, 0c etc. However, you may name them if that is more your style. The best way to proceed is to grab a pen and paper and just think about your life, from birth to today, and decide how to segment your unique Phase 0. These segments are special to you and will distinguish the important times in your life when some decision or event took you down a certain path and shaped your self-perception and subsequently your life.

The breakdown of Phase 0 will be different for everyone; sub-phases can be as short or as long as they need to be. Perhaps for you, 0–13 years of age is one big subphase; everything before you hit your teens feels like just one big memory of a loving family and a fun childhood. As a 40-year-old, perhaps a company restructure saw you unexpectedly retrenched and marks the beginning of a five year entrepreneurial journey. Perhaps you suffered a significant incident as an 8-year-old – a death in the family; your parents divorced; you won a significant academic or sporting event; or simply that you and your family moved to a new house and you started at a new school. If a single year was particularly significant to your life, distinguish it. So too with an event where you made a major life decision – did

Step 1: Discover Yourself

choosing to live with your mother rather than with your father lead you down a different path? Perhaps the decision to study film instead of law, or take a gap year and travel, sent you down a different fork in the road which brought you to where you are today. Or did the global financial crisis of 2008 force you to delay your retirement? Trust your instinct on this; you will know how to break out your own life segments, and you will know the different themes each subphase represents. Some of these will be negative, others will be positive.

Once you have broken your life history into parts, start by using dot points to explain **what** was happening in your life at this time, and **why** you have made it a segment of Phase 0. Where you can and need to, expand on each of your dot points. Lay yourself bare, and be honest about your fears, ambitions, failures and successes. Identify key decisions you made, and the people who were significant, and why they were so. If you lost these people from your life, say why.

After your dot points, include some specific memories from that period. Some memories might be general (e.g., 'every summer we spent two weeks at the beach with my cousins'; or 'my brother and I played basketball all the time in our backyard'); others will be very specific. When discussing your memories, recall the way you felt and reacted at the time of occurrence of each of them; this will help in identifying patterns and understanding why that memory is important to you.

This part may take you some time; do not rush it. The level of detail you choose to go into is up to you. The goal is to recognise and articulate the path your life has taken to bring you to where you are, so that we can plan your future. One word or one sentence may be enough for you to know why that subphase has significance; you are the only person who ever needs to read and understand it.

Example Life Map — Phase 0

Before you give it a go, let's take a look a fictional example for an individual named Jack, from birth to finishing high school. This example should give you an idea of how you can approach the next activity; however, you may be inspired to do it in a different way, and of course when doing your Phase 0 Life Map, there will be a lot more information and detail than in the example.

Jack's Phase 0

Phase 0a: 2000 – 2011: The Early Years

Age: Birth – 10 years old

Summary

- I lived with my parents and older brother. My grandparents lived in the next street.
- I started school when I was 5 years old. I liked school and had a good group of friends.

Memories

- Walking to Grandma's house and stopping at the store on the way to buy ice-cream most weekends.
- Playing in the yard with my older brother who taught me how to play soccer. I remember one weekend he spent hours tossing the ball at my head so I would learn to head butt it with my eyes open.
- Playing with my friends in the park near our house after school. We would play all sorts of sports. Sometimes we would just go exploring and climb

- trees, throw rocks in the pond, or try and catch frogs and insects.
- I remember when I was hit by a car. I was knocked from my bike while riding to school when I was 8 years old. I broke my arm and had to wear a cast at the start of the summer. It was really quite scary, but I mostly felt ashamed at my stupidity, as the accident was my fault. Wearing the cast and not being able to go swimming for the first half of the summer felt like my punishment for getting myself hit by a car.

Phase 0b: 2011 – 2013: Upheaval

Age: 10 to 12 years old

Summary:

- This period was significant as over this time Dad got a new job which meant we had to move to Melbourne.
- Mum and Dad argued a lot over this period, and I was worried they would get divorced. Things settled down about a year after our move.
- I met my best friend, Matthew, at my new school.
- I started to learn how to play the guitar.

Memories:

- My first day at my new school I was very nervous. I had grown up in a regional town and could not remember ever being in a situation where there were so many new people whom I didn't know. Luckily,

Matthew was the first person I talked to that day and we became best friends almost immediately.

Phase 0c: 2013 – 2019: High School

Age: 12 to 18 years old

Summary:

- This period was significant as it was my High School years a represents that whole time period of my life.

- I adjusted to high school pretty well. My older brother was popular, and a good sportsman and student, so it made it easy for me to settle in.

- I got into music, became obsessed with practising guitar and played in the high school band.

- There was a bad car accident when I was 14 years old, and two of my brother's friends were killed. Two others were hurt badly but recovered. My brother would have normally been with them, but my parents had made him attend a family function instead. This was a significant event for both of us, and shaped my decisions as a teenager when it came to drink driving and speeding.

- I had my first girlfriend when I was 16 and we dated for a year. We stayed friends after we broke up.

- Worked weekends and after school at McDonalds when I was 15 to 17 years old, but I quit in my final year of high school to focus on studies.

- I struggled trying to decide what to do when I finished school; I was torn between doing what was sensible (going to university) and wanting the freedom to travel and play music. I ended up being accepted into a Physiotherapy degree, but was able to take a gap year first; so, in a way I did not have to choose between them at this point.

Memories:

- The first time I played in front of an audience; the lights in my eyes, the sound of the crowd, feeling the vibrations of the music pumping through the speakers and the excitement of it all.

- Hearing about the car accident and locking eyes with my brother. The shock of realising that if he had been out with them, he might have died.

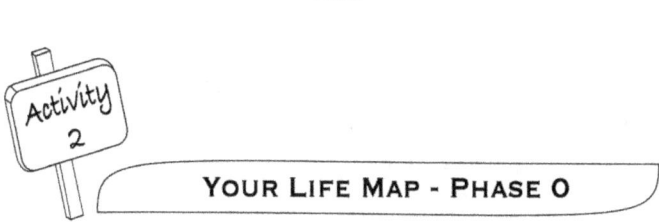

YOUR LIFE MAP - PHASE 0

Time to write your Phase 0!

There is a template for this in the appendices at the back of this book; you can download one at TakeCommandLifePlanning.com; or create your own.

1. Design your timeline based on your life subphases.
2. Write a summary for each subphase, outlining what was happening in your life during that period.

Cover basic details, such as where you lived, who you lived with, where you worked or went to school, significant relationships (family, friends and love interests).

Include any major decisions you made during that time; consider any dilemmas you faced, and how and why you made your decision. Also think about how you reacted or responded to any significant events, such as how you dealt with a break-up, winning a grand final, or missing out on a sought-after job.

3. Identify your key memories for that time period.

Include routine memories – those activities or events that occurred regularly so that the memory seems to merge (Friday Happy Hour drinks after work each week; holidaying at the same campsite each school holidays).

Include specific memories of events, which may be significant life events or simply a positive or negative memory that just sticks with you (e.g., your earliest memory; getting caught shoplifting as a teen; meeting your spouse; a specific New Years' Eve celebration).

The past is a predictor of the future

Once you have a good draft of your life to date, it is time to go back over it and objectively assess yourself. This is to unearth the person you are now, in a way that helps you understand how your past has shaped you. True self-awareness is essential to building a fulfilling and purposeful life.

The written record of details, events and memories from your past provides an opportunity to identify repeated patterns in

Step 1: Discover yourself

your thoughts and behaviours – both positive and negative. For example, do you always go on a health kick after a break-up, do you react to disappointment by running away from situations, or do you never try one hundred per cent at anything so that if things do not work out you can claim it's because you did not really try in the first place? In your thoughts, what internal dialogue accompanied you at significant events or decisions in your life? Do you recall avoiding wearing a swimsuit from a young age due to thinking you were overweight or unattractive, and recognise that those same thoughts plagued you on your wedding day? Does your jealousy of your sibling's success impact your family interactions or reduce your motivation? Have you noticed that you have been happiest in jobs where you worked in a team or had a lot of interaction with other people? There is a huge range of possibilities here, but hopefully these examples provide an illustration of what to look for.

Examining your Phase 0 Life Map is a structured way to explore these patterns in yourself. This provides an opportunity for enhanced self-awareness and personal growth. When it is laid out in front of you, it is easier to identify and recall when you were happiest, most content, or miserable, which can help you decide what you need more and less of in your life moving forward.

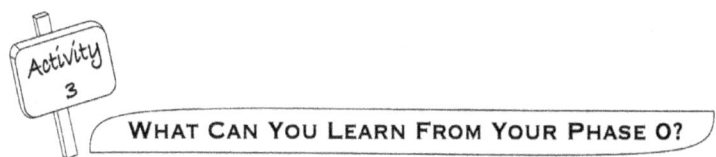

What Can You Learn From Your Phase 0?

Look back over Phase 0 of your Life Map and make note of the following:

1. What do you notice about patterns in your behaviour? Is this positive or negative? Are these patterns you would like to change or continue?

2. Do you have any regrets? What do you regret about that event or decision? What did you learn from it? If you had to do it over again, would you?

3. What are your greatest achievements to date? What made them so significant? How did it impact or change your life?

4. What are your greatest failures to date? What impact did they have on you? Did a failure push you to try again, or did you give up on that goal and move on in another direction? How did it change your life?

5. When in your life have you been the happiest and most content? Why?

6. When in your life have you felt trapped, unhappy or frustrated? Why?

Not quite finished with Step 1 just yet…

Writing about your past and analysing it is a big task. I expect you will have already begun to increase your self-awareness and started to think about how you can use this to improve your life moving forward. However, before moving on in the process, there are a few psychological concepts that can be explored. These concepts can provide some additional insight into who you are and begin to uncover your strengths and weaknesses. In the next chapter, Step 1 continues as you look at some psychological tools and tests and continue to discover yourself.

CHAPTER 3
STEP 1: DISCOVER YOURSELF – TOOLS

Know yourself and you will win all battles.
—Sun Tzu

THERE ARE MANY ways to approach self-analysis, and countless psychological and philosophical concepts on this topic that you can explore. In this book, I will discuss four psychological concepts, but this is by no means exhaustive, and there is no 'one size fits all' approach to self-discovery. If any of these concepts spark your interest, and you wish to explore further, you will find links to additional resources at: TakeCommandLifePlanning.com.

Personality testing
The Big 5

There are various personality tests that you can take to gain insight into yourself. One of the best-known is the Big 5, developed and refined over the 1980s and 90s. American psychologists Paul Costa and Robert McCrae had large numbers of participants complete various personality questionnaires; they then analysed the data to uncover clusters of traits. The findings identified the five dimensions of personality now known as the Big 5. They are:

1. **Openness**

    This relates to an individual's openness to new experiences and ideas, and includes intellectual curiosity, divergent thinking, and an active imagination. Individuals scoring highly on openness are unconventional and independent thinkers; those with low scores are more conventional, preferring the familiar to the new.

2. **Conscientiousness**

    This relates to self-discipline and control. Individuals with high scores on this factor are determined, organised, and plan for events in their lives. Individuals with low scores tend to be careless, easily distracted from their goals, or the tasks that they are undertaking.

3. **Extraversion**

    This dimension relates to sociability. Individuals with higher scores are sociable, energetic, optimistic, friendly and assertive. Individuals with low scores are reserved, sometimes shy, but they are also independent, enjoy personal reflection and working alone. An extravert will often feel energised from social interactions; introverts can often feel drained by them.

4. **Agreeableness**

   This measures an individual's inclination for social interaction. High scorers are trusting, helpful, soft-hearted and sympathetic. Those with low scores are suspicious, antagonistic, unhelpful, sceptical and uncooperative.

5. **Neuroticism (emotional stability)**

   This relates to emotional stability and personal adjustment. An individual who scores highly on neuroticism experiences wide mood swings and is volatile in their emotions. Individuals with low scores on the neuroticism factor are calm, well-adjusted and good at regulating their emotions.

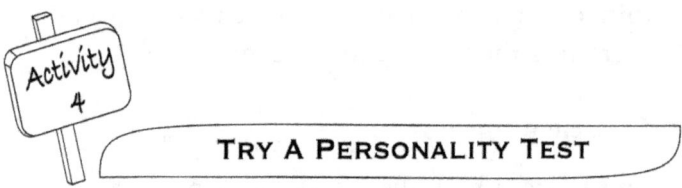

TRY A PERSONALITY TEST

Take some time to try a personality test and see what you learn about yourself. Conduct an internet search or visit TakeCommandLifePlanning.com for links to various online personality tests. There is the Big 5, which has been described; however, there are many others that have been developed. Several other popular ones include the 16 Personality Factor Questionnaire and Myers–Briggs Type Indicator.

Cognitive dissonance

Cognitive dissonance occurs where you experience a conflict between your beliefs, attitudes and/or behaviour. Humans tend to seek consistency; when we experience cognitive dissonance, we feel discomfort and the need to reduce or eliminate conflict. This can be rectified through a change in behaviour or belief; however, the more likely response is to create justifications, explanations or excuses.

Take as an example, a man who feels guilt at consuming animal products because of the industrialised methods and techniques that an animal experiences before it becomes a Sunday roast, or provides the milk in his coffee. He may experience a cognitive dissonance between his desire for steak and his knowledge of the trauma that the animal felt before bits of it ended up on his plate. To alleviate his discomfort, he could change his behaviour and choose either to reduce or completely cease consumption of animal products, or he could justify his decision to not change his dietary choices. He can leverage his belief that eating animal products is essential for optimal human health, or perhaps that it is inconvenient, time consuming and expensive pursuing a vegetarian or vegan lifestyle. However, it is likely he will continue to experience a level of discomfort between his behaviour and beliefs. If he does not change his behaviour, he will regularly need to reinforce his decision with a justification.

Other common examples of cognitive dissonance relate to bad habits, such as smoking cigarettes when you know they are bad for your health, or being tempted by junk food when you are on a diet and actively trying to lose weight. You can experience dissonance if you believe you need to reduce your waste to benefit the environment, but you continue to use single-use plastics and do not recycle. In a workplace, your supervisor may ask you to perform a task that you know is ethically questionable, or a workplace hazard, but you perform the task anyway. A more severe example is where a neighbour may have a belief that a child is being abused by a parent or caregiver, but feel unable to take any action. They may attempt to nullify or diminish their suspicion, however will likely continue to feel unease over their inaction.

Cognitive dissonance is ultimately a mechanism by which we can identify a mismatch between our belief system and our behaviours. As an indicator that something is not aligned within ourself, it can present a positive opportunity for growth and change. However, it can be detrimental when you rationalise destructive or negative beliefs or behaviours (such as addictions, or aggressive or criminal behaviour) or the dissonance causes you excessive stress.

To rectify or eliminate cognitive dissonance, where possible take action to change either your mindset or your behaviours. Although the default assumption is that it is the behaviour that needs to change, it may be that a belief is the cause of the dissonance. An example – a conservative politician who has an anti-LGBTQ agenda but engages in a same-sex sexual relationship. His suppression of his true feelings is at odds with his behaviour. He will likely never shake the cognitive dissonance he experiences until he adjusts his beliefs to align with his behaviour, which is a natural expression of his true self as a gay man.

Even if you find a disconnect between a belief system and behaviour that you cannot change (or are unable to in the short term), at least be aware that it exists so that you have greater awareness and control over the impact it may have on your wellbeing.

Do You Experience Cognitive Dissonance?

Is there any cognitive dissonance creating friction in your life?

It may be difficult to identify cognitive dissonance by simply recalling aspects of your day-to-day life. Now that you know about cognitive dissonance, you may find that you can identify it when you experience it, and you can take action when it happens in future. However, for now, using the range of examples provided, consider when you have experienced it in the past, and whether it is something that you continue to experience.

Once you have identified a cognitive dissonance, consider how it is affecting you: do you just feel discomfort? Or is it causing you stress and anxiety? Contemplate whether it is your beliefs or your behaviours that need to change, and which choice is best for your wellbeing. Decide which of the following options you can take to reduce or eliminate your cognitive dissonance:

1. Change your beliefs.
2. Change your behaviours.
3. Determine a justification that reconciles the dissonance between your beliefs and behaviours.

Self-esteem vs self-efficacy

Here is another concept you might like to consider: self-efficacy and self-esteem. Most people are familiar with the term **self-esteem**: it describes the level of respect or sense of worth one has for themselves. However, most people are probably less familiar with the term **self-efficacy**, a concept first developed by psychologist Albert Bandura. Self-efficacy is a part of self-esteem, specifically describing the belief one has in their ability to succeed, and their perceived level of competence. Understanding your levels of self-esteem and self-efficacy can assist you in gaining greater self-awareness.

People with healthy self-esteem will be confident and assertive about expressing their opinions; they form strong relationships and are resilient and realistic about their virtues and flaws. They will feel good about themselves and feel worthy and deserving of respect. Those prone to low self-esteem tend to focus on their faults, be overly self-critical, have low self-worth, and have difficulty accepting positive feedback. The effects of low self-esteem can result in someone staying in an abusive relationship, or not retaliating when being bullied or harassed. They could also have problems with body image, or resort to addictive behaviours as a method of coping with feelings of inadequacy.

Those who have high self-efficacy are confident in their ability to perform well and succeed in various situations. They are likely to view challenging tasks positively, seeing them as opportunities to master a new skill; they have resilience to failure and recover from setbacks quickly. Those with poor self-efficacy have little faith in their abilities and will avoid challenging tasks; they tend to focus on their personal failings. Someone with low self-efficacy is less likely to seek a promotion or pay rise, so could stay in a low-level job despite having the skills and experience to progress. If facing a health challenge, those with low self-efficacy are more likely to give up at the first obstacle, which could affect their recovery and rehabilitation. An individual who has high self-efficacy, newly diagnosed with Type 2 diabetes, will probably have the confidence and resilience to persist with changes to their lifestyle that could reverse the diagnosis. Conversely, having low self-efficacy could result in failure to even attempt improving their prognosis.

From these descriptions it is easy to see why it is generally accepted that people are either high or low in both self-esteem and self-efficacy, as there are parallels between them. However, this is not always the case. Self-esteem is confidence in our 'being'; self-efficacy is confidence in our 'doing'. So, it is possible for people to have low self-esteem and yet high self-efficacy (or the other way around).

Low self-esteem and high self-efficacy can be associated with perfectionists; such a person will likely be negative and overly critical of themselves in some respects, but also see themselves as highly competent. Perhaps a brilliant lawyer, who can command authority in a courtroom, has no confidence in herself as a woman, and has low self-worth, due to her upbringing, combined with several failed relationships. This woman has no doubt about her professional skill (high self-efficacy); however, she feels inadequate in personal relationships (low self-esteem). As a result, she invests even more time in her work, which sets her in a spiral that keeps her at the top of her career, but facilitates her avoidance of personal relationships, reinforcing her feelings of personal failure and low self-worth.

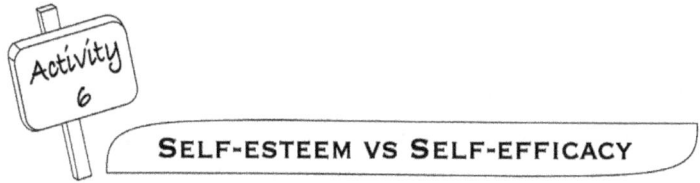

SELF-ESTEEM VS SELF-EFFICACY

How high is your self-esteem and self-efficacy?

Take a moment to do both a self-esteem and a self-efficacy test. Keep in mind that questionnaires measuring self-esteem also measure self-efficacy, and this can skew results. However, there are questionnaires that measure self-efficacy distinct from the broader category of self-esteem, so if you do both types of test, you may find the results interesting and insightful.

Two questionnaires are included in the appendices at the end of this book so that you can assess your self-esteem and self-efficacy. You can also find resources at TakeCommandLifePlanning.com or try an internet search of your own.

What do your results reveal?

Self-discrepancy theory

Another approach you can use to explore your sense of self is Higgins' Self-Discrepancy Theory. This theory proposes that there are three different domains of self:

1. Actual Self: The attributes that you believe you **do** possess (belief).

2. Ideal Self: The attributes you **want to** possess (aspirational).

3. Ought Self: The attributes you believe you **should or ought to** possess (duty/obligation).

Teenagers and young adults can often feel tension between their different selves as they question the world around them and seek to find their identity. A teenager may think of their Actual Self as being inadequate in some way – not being attractive enough, or smart enough. This teenager could have an ideal image of themselves as an adult working in the fashion industry and looking like a supermodel. This same teenager could feel pressure from their parents to excel academically at school and pursue a career as a doctor. The pressures and feelings of inadequacy would undoubtedly cause stress and despondency.

Such tensions are not restricted to youth: someone older could feel their Actual Self is a reliable mother and partner, their Ideal Self is a free spirit with no responsibilities, and their Ought Self is the stereotypical superwoman who effortlessly juggles their responsibilities, always has a gleaming home, and polite, well-behaved children. Someone in their retirement may feel a bit lost or unhappy when they first leave the workforce, which conflicts with the beliefs of their Ideal Self as being joyful at finally having ample time to indulge their hobbies, or their Ought Self as looking after grandchildren, or volunteering. So, regardless of age and where you are in your life, you may find conflict between these three domains of self.

There are characteristic emotions associated with discrepancies between Actual Self and either of Ideal or Ought Self. For example, if your Actual Self and Ideal Self are not aligned, you can experience disappointment and despondency. If there is conflict between your Actual Self and Ought Self, you may feel guilty, stressed or anxious. Understanding where discrepancy exists can assist you in working towards self-improvement; where your Ideal or Ought Self sets unrealistic expectations, you can seek to reduce or nullify any detrimental negative emotional impacts. Becoming aware of any such malalignment may also provide insight into your thoughts, beliefs and behaviours.

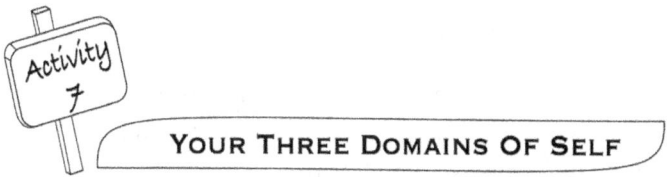

Activity 7 — Your Three Domains Of Self

It is now time to explore your three domains of self, and then consider if any discrepancy between them is causing you any stress or despondency.

1. Describe your Actual Self.

This is the way you see yourself now: what kind of person are you? What traits and attributes do you possess? How would you describe yourself?

2. Describe your Ideal Self.

This is aspirational; when you imagine your 'perfect' self, what traits do you have? How does this version of you differ from your Actual Self? How does this discrepancy make you feel? What can you do to alleviate any negative feelings that arise over this discrepancy?

3. Describe your Ought Self.

This is tied to a sense of duty or obligation. What traits do you think you should possess? What kind of person do you think you should be? How does this version of you differ from your Actual Self? How does this discrepancy make you feel? What can you do to alleviate any negative feelings that arise over this discrepancy?

Step 1 Summary

You have now completed Step 1! Going over your past and drilling down into the depths of who you are can be exhausting and emotional, but also rewarding.

Hopefully creating Phase 0 of your Life Map and examining some psychological concepts and tools has been useful to you in identifying patterns of behaviour or gaining a greater depth of understanding about how you might be holding yourself back

Step 1: Discover yourself — Tools

from fulfilling your potential. Some patterns you may not be able to 'fix'; however, knowing that they exist, and being able to recognise these thought and behaviour patterns, will allow you to either intervene when they occur, minimise the damage they can cause, or at very least be compassionate and understanding towards yourself when you recognise them. It is inescapable that we all have weaknesses; the important thing is to know what they are and how they impact you, so that you have greater control over your responses and decisions and reduce your vulnerability to self-sabotage. However, this is not about just focusing on the negative. Hopefully you have also been able to gain greater clarity and insight into your strengths, so that you can find ways to maximise your as you move towards greater self-awareness.

However well you thought you knew yourself before lifting up this book, I hope you have discovered something more about yourself, or have gained insight into how aspects of your past have led you to where you are today. In Step 2, we will bring together what we have learnt from Step 1 and turn this growing awareness into tools to sharpen your focus and decide how you want your life to be.

> **Step 1 Outcomes**
> Activity 1: Your Life Right Now
> Activity 2: Your Life Map - Phase 0
> Activity 3: What Can You Learn From Your Phase 0?
> Activity 4: Try A Personality Test
> Activity 5: Do You Experience Cognitive Dissonance?
> Activity 6: Self-esteem Vs Self-efficacy
> Activity 7: Your Three Domains Of Self

CHAPTER 4
STEP 2: UNCOVER WHAT DRIVES YOU

To the person who does not know where he wants to go there is no favourable wind.
—Seneca

NOW YOU HAVE conducted some self-exploration, it is time to take this to the next level: self-realisation and uncovering your Life Drivers. In Step 2 you will summarise what you have discovered from Step 1 by articulating your Vulnerability and Capability Statements. You will also consider your beliefs and approach to life by articulating your Life Philosophy. Then, you will step through an activity to uncover and formulate your enduring Life Drivers. Whether you realise it or not, you already have drivers that influence almost all decisions you make and shape you towards your life destination. Understanding these drivers will help you frame what is important in your life and may also help you discover why you have taken a certain path – for better or worse. It is important to realise that you may have drivers that are not helpful to you.

The work you do in this step will get at the heart of who you are and what you want out of your life. Your Life Philosophy and your Life Drivers are the pillars that hold your purpose and happiness; being true to them in how you live your life will ensure you find fulfillment and contentment.

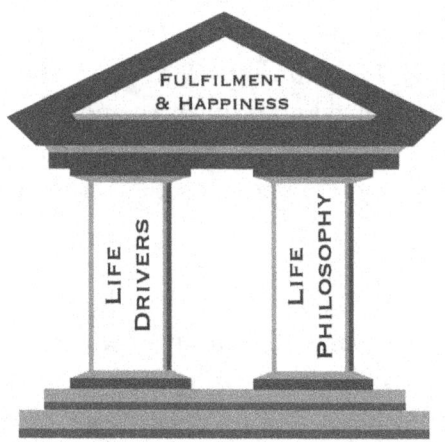

Vulnerability and Capability Statements

Having a clear, level-headed understanding of both your strengths and vulnerabilities helps with self-awareness, identifies opportunities for development, and allows for self-compassion. In writing both Vulnerability and Capability Statements, the goal is to produce a statement that is matter of fact, objective and non-derogatory.

Let's begin with Vulnerability Statements, and launch straight into two examples:

- I tend to behave in ways that push people away from me. I am introverted and do not like sharing my feelings. My low self-efficacy means I often feel like an imposter at work, despite being successful, and this combination can provoke periods of isolating myself from others and overindulging in alcohol.

- My high self-esteem and high self-efficacy make me vulnerable to arrogance and dismissiveness in my dealings with others. A conflict exists between my Actual Self and Ought Self, and I am vulnerable to feelings of anxiety and stress as a result. My high expectations mean I work excessive hours, push myself to exhaustion and reduce my ability to have meaningful relationships with my partner and children. My behaviour also has the potential to negatively influence my children, who are high-achievers and also prone to stress and self-imposed high expectations.

As you can see from these examples, the goal here is to lay bare the negative aspects of ourselves, without using hateful or judgemental language, focusing on patterns of behaviours and thoughts. Details about personal appearance, or financial and social status, are irrelevant, as the goal is to understand the aspects of our internal self, not our outward projection, that can hinder us in achieving the life we deserve.

YOUR VULNERABILITY STATEMENT

Looking back over the work you have done in Step 1, draft a statement that summarises, in a matter of fact, objective and non-derogatory way, your **weaknesses**, focusing on vulnerabilities in your thoughts and behaviours.

Step 2: Uncover what drives you

Now let us move on and look at the Capability Statement. It is basically the same process as writing a Vulnerability Statement, with a focus on your **strengths**.

If we use the previous two examples, here are example capability statements that complement them:

- I am a high achiever, who is humble and thankful for the opportunities I have had in my life, and proud that I had the fortitude to maximise them. Being introverted, good at working independently, and also being conscientious, allows me to excel in my chosen field. I am a go-getter with an open mind who will work hard, and I do not take people or my success for granted. I am a good listener and a good friend. I am also generous and kind.

- I am strong and capable, and I put my family's needs above my own. I will make sacrifices to ensure they have everything they need. I am a good and attentive parent. I am an extravert and can be funny and witty which makes people like to be around me. I am intelligent and flexible in my thinking, which helps me excel at work. I have high energy levels, which gives me the capacity to achieve more in my day than others.

Once again, you will see the language needs to be objective and focused on characteristics and behaviours, not on status, assets or appearance. This is not to brag or be narcissistic, it is simply objectively identifying your strengths. Taking the emotion out of these statements increases their significance and highlights your truth. Remember that these statements are private and solely for your benefit; you do not need to share these with anyone else. Be as honest and direct as you can.

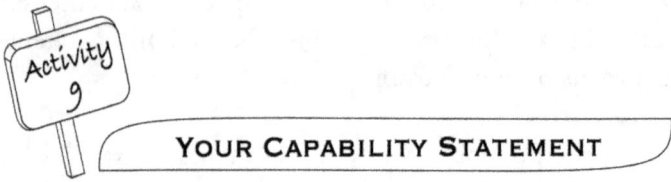

Your Capability Statement

Looking back over the work you have done in Step 1, draft a statement that summarises your **strengths**, focusing on capabilities in your thoughts and behaviours, in a matter of fact, objective and humble way.

Life Philosophy

Having a Life Philosophy can benefit you by helping you articulate what is important to you in the way that you live your life, and what you want out of it. It can generate motivation and provide you with a greater sense of fulfilment as it helps you determine your path.

When considering your own Life Philosophy, it is important to think beyond your religion (if you are a believer) and ensure that you personalise your Life Philosophy. Whether devoutly religious or an atheist, you will have a belief system and a certain approach to your life that is uniquely yours. People draw on a range of sources in developing their approach to life and it is often shaped by parents and families as they grow from childhood; learning the values of right and wrong from the world they live in. The belief systems, creeds, cultures and subcultures you are exposed to from your childhood, through adolescence and adulthood will all play a part in shaping your

Step 2: Uncover what drives you

Life Philosophy. Whether you accept or reject what you are exposed to, nonetheless it is influencing your personal beliefs.

Religion means something different and personal to each individual. Some may be practising and devout, with religion forming a significant part of their life and identity. Others may identify as, for example, a Catholic, but go to that church only once or twice a year, and then only for family events. Many people will have a Life Philosophy that extends beyond just their religious views and will need to consider the broader aspects of their belief system. Those who are not religious may draw on aspects of different religious concepts from either their cultural background or other spiritually based inspiration, such as 'an eye for an eye', charity, personal sacrifice, or karma.

There are a range of other concepts, beyond religion, that could form the foundation of someone's Life Philosophy. You can draw inspiration from philosophical concepts, political or environmental views, or a stance on ethical food consumption or other significant lifestyle choice. Some people feel drawn to particular sayings or catch phrases, which seem to encapsulate their Life Philosophy, such as the acronym YOLO (you only live once); or 'what goes around, comes around'. If you do have a tendency or fondness for a particular saying or phase, you may benefit from considering its significance to you and your beliefs. All of these concepts can form the backbone of a Life Philosophy.

To provoke some thought and perhaps identify themes that resonate with you, here are a few different types of philosophical concepts that may help you articulate your Life Philosophy:

Humanism

Humanism is a rational philosophy that, without theism or other supernatural beliefs, affirms that humanity must take responsibility for its own destiny and aspire to the greater good. It recognises that humans are a part of nature and that we have the ability to lead ethical lives with moral values founded on human nature and experience alone, free from supernaturalism.

Existentialism

Similar to Humanism, Existentialism also espouses individual choice and free will. Under this philosophy, people can find their own meaning of life in an irrational world. However, while the Humanist believes that people are intrinsically good, Existentialists do not assume that people are either good or bad, and sees the potential for both great good and evil within human nature.

Stoicism

Founded in Ancient Greece and also practised in Ancient Rome, Stoicism asserts that humans should aspire to maintain tranquillity or equilibrium, rather than being at the mercy of bursts of irrational emotion. With many parallels to Buddhism, Stoicism is concerned with the concept of control, in that we have control only over our thoughts – nothing more. Indeed, we do not even have control over our bodies, which can be ravaged by disease or illness. Stoics believe that our happiness depends on the view we choose to take in any situation, and the realisation that every situation could always be worse. For example, if someone insults you, it is your decision whether you actually feel insulted and whether you allow yourself to feel angry or upset, or if you ignore it, feel amused by it, or pity the person for having to harbour such ill intent. James Bond Stockdale, a Medal of

Step 2: Uncover what drives you

Honour recipient, credited his perseverance and survival as a POW during the Vietnam War to the Stoic philosophy.

A final word on writing your Life Philosophy Statement – it can be as long or as short as you like. You could write a sentence, a paragraph, or a list of dot points, or you might favour creating a montage of images. Here are a few examples of Life Philosophy statements:

- You have one life to live, so live it. Fill your cup with as much experience you can squeeze from the world. Live with an open heart, do not let envy or pain shut you down. Live your own way and do not let the judgement of others change your course.

- Trust in God's love to guide you and give you strength. Do not talk about it, do it. And when you fail, persist.

- Live to seek maximum personal enjoyment while minimising disruption to others. Demonstrate happiness, kindness and love.

- Work hard, play hard. Strive to be the best in whatever you put your mind to. Love and live without fear.

- Do no harm, leave the world better than you found it and enjoy the journey!

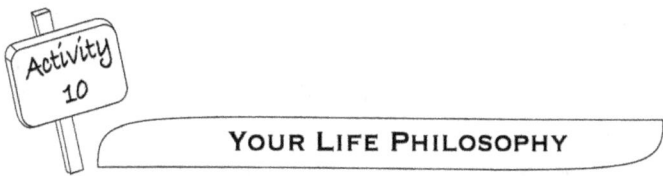

Activity 10: Your Life Philosophy

You now can write a statement that encapsulates your Life Philosophy. Using a statement, paragraph, dot points, images, whatever format you desire – write down what best describes your belief system and your approach to life.

Life Drivers

Life Drivers are those key beliefs that sit at the heart of all major decisions and essentially 'drive' you towards certain people, places and activities throughout the course of your life. Even in circumstances where we have no idea what is driving us, we will still be making decisions and holding a moral line that is reflective of a fundamental belief about the world and/or ourselves.

When I was first exploring how to create a Life Plan, a good friend of mine, who was also writing a Life Plan, shared her concept of drivers. I could see parallels to the concept of core values, which is popular in life-coaching circles; however, I found that the idea of Life Drivers resonated with me far more. My friend stepped me through the process to help me uncover my drivers. We sat at a whiteboard as she questioned me, and helped me identify recurring themes that had formed the basis of my past decisions and motivations. As we talked and I explained myself, or corrected her interpretation of my answers, I was able to identify and then refine the wording of my Life Drivers.

In my initial draft, I had identified four drivers; however, as I worked on rewriting them and ensuring I was capturing the essence of what they were, I realised that two of them were actually covering the same concept. At the end of the process, the three Life Drivers that I uncovered revolutionised my understanding of myself and what I truly wanted out of my life. It was not that I had been completely unaware of these underlying motivations; however, articulating exactly what they were increased

Step 2: Uncover what drives you

my awareness of their significance in driving my decisions and behaviour, even when I did not realise it was occurring. I also gained clarity on when my drivers had previously caused conflict in decision making, where an outcome favoured one driver at the expense of another. Just about everything I had done in my life could be traced back to one of those three intrinsic motivations.

The Life Drivers I uncovered all have their origins in my childhood; however, others may find they have drivers that materialised at different times in their life after significant life events. For example, someone might find or lose their faith in a certain religion, have a near-death or significant life experience, or simply have a major shift in their views as an adult, prompting the development of new drivers. It is also worth considering if your existing drivers require modification as you move through life; a driver about the importance of family may need to be expanded as your family grows or it may prompt the creation of a new Life Driver.

Something to be cautious of when uncovering your Life Drivers, is not to confuse them with goals. Life Drivers are not 'goals' to be achieved, although some people may find if they are particularly passionate about something it may be entwined with a major career or life goal. It may help to think of your Life Driver as the bowstring that powers the arrow's flight, and your goal is a target. In fact, each Life Driver will probably have multiple goals or milestones it could aim for. If you do find a major life goal embedded in one of your drivers, do your best to distinguish your Life Driver (such as a passion for music) from your goal (being a professional singer).

It is also important to understand that Life Drivers can either have a positive or negative influence over your decision making. A good example is a Life Driver centred on finding a soulmate or 'the One'. This could be positive in motivating an individual towards meeting a partner and committing to a happy, lifelong relationship. However, it could drive someone to make decisions that result in negative consequences. It could lead someone to pursue unhealthy or toxic relationships in their overwhelming desire to be coupled. Such an individual would rather be in bad relationship than single. Alternatively, a different type of person may be driven to set unrealistic expectations and be constantly disappointed in partners who cannot live up to their idealistic vision, prematurely ending otherwise promising relationships. Another possible scenario could lead someone to put their life on hold if their drive to be in a relationship is tied to some of their major life goals, such as travelling the world, buying a home or starting a family. If 'the One' fails to materialise by a certain age, this type of individual may start to feel that they have missed the boat, letting their life pass by without fulfilling their other aspirations which they had planned on doing only once they had met their soulmate.

As you can see from the examples, understanding what your Life Drivers are and how they influence your decisions – both positively and negatively – will give you the ability to make deliberate and informed choices.

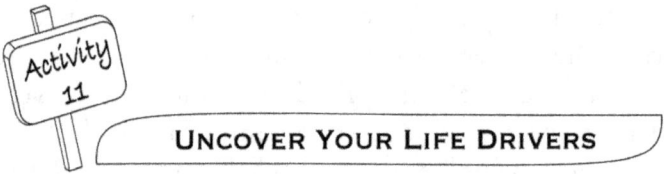

UNCOVER YOUR LIFE DRIVERS

This activity is a big one! Some people may fly through it, others may take some time.

1. Look back over Phase 0 of your Life Map to identify major life decisions and significant events that have prompted a response or reaction from you.

STEP 2: UNCOVER WHAT DRIVES YOU

2. Note down any other significant decisions or events not covered in your Phase 0 that have impacted the direction of your life and note them in your Life Map.

3. Answer these questions:

- What is it that motivates you to take a certain action, or make decisions? For each major decision you have made, ask yourself:
  - What factors were important when making this decision / causing this event?
  - Was there conflict in your ability to make the decision? If so, what was the conflict?
  - What were your emotional responses to needing to make the decision, and the decision itself, once it was made?
  - How did you behave or respond to the situation once it had resolved?

- What is the worst decision you ever made?
  - Why did you make it? (e.g., for money? Out of Ambition? For Love?).
  - What was it that blinded you from making the right choice in this circumstance?
  - Did you make that decision because you wanted something, even though you knew it might be a mistake?
  - What do you regret about that decision?
  - Given your time over, would you do it again? Was the experience and consequences worth it? (e.g., a bad relationship giving you the gift of your child.)

- What does this tell you about yourself and your motivations?
* What was the best decision you ever made?
    - What knowledge or information was necessary in making this decision?
    - Could it have turned bad, or were you confident it would turn out well?
    - Why did you make it (i.e., for money, love, ambition)? Why was it a good decision?
    - What does this tell you about yourself and your motivations?
* What are your favourite sayings? What does this reveal about you?
* What is something you are renowned for doing or saying? What does that tell you about yourself?
* What do you want, more than anything in your life? (You can have multiple answers.)
* Is there something missing in your life that you have been striving for but have not been able to achieve?

4. Reviewing your responses to the questions so far, try to identify recurring themes and patterns in the way you approach decision making, and in your reactions to events. Such recurring themes may indicate that this is an underlying motivation and may reveal one or more of your drivers.

Below are some different themes to evoke some ideas; however, this list is by no means exhaustive!

Step 2: Uncover what drives you

> **Wellbeing**   *Love*   health   teaching
> **adventure**   Challenge   Success
>   *family*   exploration   belonging
> **Growth**   Wealth   *Creativity*
>   sacrifice   tribe   LEARNING
> accomplishment   discovery   contentment
>   comfort   respect   humour   integrity

5. Once you have identified some themes, expand on this further to create an initial draft list of your drivers and begin to refine and articulate exactly what they are. You can start this even if you are not sure you have them quite right. Working at refining the wording and finding the best expression or description of each driver will assist in capturing what it really means to you. This is part of the process; identifying exactly what your Life Drivers are, and that the way you have expressed them speaks to you. In doing this exercise, you may realise that what you thought was one driver is actually two, or conversely that what you think are two different drivers are ultimately aspects of the same one. For example, you may find a relationship driver is better combined with a family driver as you may find your actual Life Driver is to be a part of a loving family which can be achieved either with or without a partner.

There are various ways you can articulate your Life Drivers: write them as a statement, a single word or a phrase, or an entire paragraph – whatever is needed to articulate exactly what it is that drives **you**. Here are some examples of drivers and ways to articulate them:

- Adventure.

- Finding my soulmate and have family always around me. I want a life where I am a part of a close community.

- I need to succeed, to have status and be respected.

- Fulfilling my potential to achieve success (my idea of success, not societal expectation) and making the most out of my life.

- YOLO: Travelling the world, trying new things, not wasting my life waiting.

- Financial security and independence.

- All sentient life deserves to be respected.

- I want to be a mother. If I cannot have children of my own, I will adopt, foster or find some other way have children in my life.

- Creativity and innovation – fill my world with art and beauty.

- Everything I do needs to support my family / children as best as possible.

- Survival. Whatever life throws at me, I will find a way to survive.

6. Lastly, finalise your list of Life Drivers in priority order for which is most important to you right now. The order will almost certainly change over the course of your life; however, knowing what driver is more important to you at any one time will help you make the right decision.

   Knowing your Life Drivers is just one aspect of uncovering them. Another is identifying which one is more important at any one time. You may notice, looking back at your Phase 0 record, that different motivations were driving you during different phases of your life. Perhaps a driver for adventure has given way to a driver for financial security or family? Your adventure driver may still exist, it will just be less likely to motivate a decision to choose between climbing a mountain in Nepal over being at home on your child's birthday. Understanding your drivers and knowing which ones are most important at each phase of your life will assist you in understanding why you made past decisions and help you make the best decisions in the future suitable to your current priorities. Throughout your life you will need to be aware which driver takes priority in your decision making.

Step 2 Summary

Well done! Step 2 is perhaps the hardest in this process. True self-awareness – knowing what we want out of our life, our purpose – is something that people have struggled with since the dawn of time. Do not be afraid to continue to question yourself, and further refine your Vulnerability and Capability Statements, your Life Philosophy and, of course, your Life Drivers.

We now take one final step of Take Stock, as you examine the world around you.

> **STEP 2 OUTCOMES**
> ACTIVITY 8: YOUR VULNERABILITY STATEMENT
> ACTIVITY 9: YOUR CAPABILITY STATEMENT
> ACTIVITY 10: YOUR LIFE PHILOSOPHY
> ACTIVITY 11: UNCOVER YOUR LIFE DRIVERS

CHAPTER 5
STEP 3: UNCOVER YOUR WORLD

The people you surround yourself with influence your behaviours, so choose friends who have healthy habits.
—Dan Buettner, author *Blue Zones*

THE FINAL STEP for Take Stock is to understand the world around you and how it influences you. Knowing yourself is essential, but you do not exist in isolation; our environment and the people around us all have an impact upon our lives and decisions. As you progress through this step, you will see that there is ample research exploring how what and who is in our life can shape and influence us significantly.

In a military context, this step is sometimes known as Battlespace Analysis. It is important to note that the 'Battlespace' does not consist of just the physical domain; in addition, we must

Step 3: Uncover your world

also consider the stakeholder and information space, and how these domains impact our lives.

For our Life Map, to uncover your world in Step 3 we will examine the following domains:

1. **Stakeholder** – includes your family, friends, work colleagues and pets. However, stakeholders are not just individuals, they are also groups and organisations; such as your employer, place of worship, social and community groups.
2. **Physical** – relates to your home, where you live, where you work or study, places you visit regularly or travel to, as well as how you get around (car, public transport).
3. **Information** – encompasses ideas and communication, including social media, gaming, TV, movies and hobbies.

In this step, you need to identify and accept those things that impact you, physically, spiritually and emotionally, that you cannot change or control. This is essential, because you must be realistic and accept those aspects of your world you cannot control before you can commence developing your plan. If you want to take your life down a certain path, you need to understand what it will take to get there, and determine whether you can accept the sacrifices needed.

This is also an opportunity to identify the elements in your life that you **can** control, that you do not want or have outgrown? What power do you have to effect change? For example, do you have the ability to remove a toxic relationship or unfulfilling job from your life? Perhaps you may not be able to make needed changes in the next month or year, but by building your plan you may find a way to move beyond them eventually. Alternatively, do you need to accept, for now, the toxic and the unfulfilling, and find ways to mitigate or lessen their negative impact on you? For example, if you have a toxic family member whom you cannot remove from your life, you will need to identify ways to mitigate any negative impact they have on you. Understanding how the external world influences you is the key to learning how to mitigate its impact.

To understand your world, look at the influences around you; focus on how the world external to you shapes your decisions and behaviour. Completing this step will identify habits you have developed in what you do and whom you do it with. Insight is essential to making active and deliberate decisions; that is why half this book is devoted to personal discovery, insight and self-analysis.

Stakeholder domain – I'll have what he's having

It is widely understood that the people we spend time with do influence us – for better and worse. Parents have for aeons been concerned about their children's choice of friends; about that one kid they perceive to be a bad influence. There is ample scientific research demonstrating the power of social influence, for example, the influence that parents have on their child's future life choices, peer influence on a teenager's risky behaviour, the likelihood of someone lapsing back into addiction, or more generally how an individual's health can be impacted, positively or negatively, by their friends and family.

The first major influence in our lives is that of our parents. If you are a parent, it is worth remembering how much influence you have over your child – consciously and unconsciously. Regardless of the 'nature versus nurture' debate (how much

Step 3: Uncover your world

our genes are responsible versus how much our environment is responsible for how we turn out), our environment, and the people around us, have a significant influence on us. Your personality, your opinions and your behaviour are all shaped by those closest to you, particularly parents prior to your reaching adolescence. No matter how much of an individual or how divergent you think you are, you are nonetheless influenced by, and shaped by, people you are exposed to regularly.

As we grow out of childhood, our peers become a more significant influence whose collective effect generally surpasses that of our parents. In adolescence, we usually seek to discover our identity as an individual, as distinct from the role we have in our families – such as being the smart or sporty sibling. This is prompted by a remodelling of the adolescent brain: physical changes increase the efficacy of the brain, allowing neurons to communicate with improved coordination and speed. These changes see the development of greater complexity in thinking, including abstract thinking, and increased capacity for considering alternative points of view. This makes it possible for you to more readily imagine what others may be thinking about you. Remodelling of the adolescent brain explains some of the changes in personality that occur at this time, with preoccupation with peer approval and search for identity and purpose. Questioning previously accepted norms and the authority of parents often result in adolescents being more heavily influenced by peers.

Whether it be peers or family, the influence of those around us does not diminish as we move into adulthood. Ultimately, the people you spend the most time with undoubtedly influence your beliefs, opinions and lifestyle choices. This can occur by your adopting – consciously or subconsciously – views or behaviours similar to or aligned with those of the people close to you. As you share ideas, thoughts and opinions, your point of view may shift to incorporate aspects of what you hear and learn from others. If a close friend has a strong negative opinion about a particular model of car, you will be less likely to consider it as an option for yourself. This social influence is also commonly associated with the need for our family or close friends to approve new romantic interests; disapproval could result in the decision not to pursue a relationship. Sometimes this influence falls in line with the old saying, 'if she jumped off a bridge, would you do it too?' A more apt example would be, 'if he is having dessert after dinner, then would you have it too?' People's decision to have one more drink, or to eat fast food rather than healthy food, is often swayed by what the group chooses to do. If no one else at the dinner table is having dessert, then you are less likely to order it for yourself.

Even small decisions – spending money on lunch when you are trying to budget, or skipping a gym session – have the potential to develop into habits and patterns of behaviour or thought. Encouragement from friends, colleagues and family to persist in good or bad habits can have longer-term effects on your choices, whether about health, money, lifestyle, or even whom to vote for. When you are developing your Life Plan, understanding the impacts that the people around you can have on your choices will help you make sure you are following the path you want for yourself.

This does not mean you must consider removing from your life people who have different beliefs or behaviours. There is a marked difference between people in your life who are toxic and those who simply differ in non-toxic ways. As an example, many teetotallers have close friends and family who drink alcohol. They are clear in their own path to not consume alcohol, due to religious or health reasons, or simply personal preference; they can resist being influenced to partake. The goal is to understand what you want, identify stakeholders in your life who have a positive or negative influence on your life choices, assess the level of their influence over you, and if necessary, devise ways to lessen or leverage their influence. A good option is to identify triggers and develop strategies to employ when triggered, such as walking away, repeating a mantra, or avoiding particular activities or situations. If you are seeking to reduce other people's bad influence over your health choices, plan a catch-up that does not involve sharing foods or alcohol, or take your own. If someone in your life poses an obstacle, have a frank conversation with them about your concerns, in a calm and non-argumentative way to help them understand your position.

Stakeholders are not just the human beings in your life. There are a few other stakeholders we need to consider.

Pets

It would be remiss not to discuss pets. For many, our furry friends are central to our lives. They bring us joy, comfort, and unconditional love. They also depend on us; when they share in our lives, we need to consider their needs, and how our lifestyle decisions will impact them. Having pets improves health and mood by reducing blood pressure, easing loneliness and forcing human owners to get outside and exercise regularly. That said, pets do come with responsibility; any owner also knows that pets come with mess, stress and cost. Pet ownership is a commitment for the whole lifetime of that cute puppy, kitten or other little creature – something that pet rescue organisations consistently remind people about before adoption. So, considering the influence your furry friends have on your life and lifestyle is necessary when looking holistically at your stakeholders.

Organisations

There are organisations that are often stakeholders in our lives. A major one for me, for example, is the Army – a huge stakeholder and influencer in my life. Those who serve, and their families, often refer to the Army, or the military more broadly, in a manner that can indicate it is its own self-determining entity. Long work hours and work travel might provoke someone to claim 'the Army is destroying my marriage', as if the Army is a person with a deliberate intention to cause their marriage breakdown. In this way, you can see how an organisation can take on the role of a human entity. Other examples: your employer, the bank, the government, a place of worship, or volunteer or social organisations. Such organisations can be important stakeholders because they have a tangible influence in our lives that can impact us positively and negatively. We cannot discount the influence an organisational stakeholder has on your life and wellbeing. Perhaps there is no such significant organisation influencing your life, but if there is one, this will resonate with you; you will understand how impactful such an entity can be on your life.

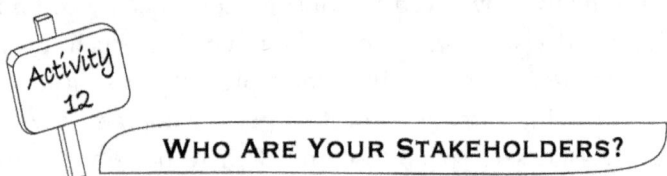

Activity 12 — WHO ARE YOUR STAKEHOLDERS?

It is now time to consider your stakeholders.

Write a list, or you could create a mind map, of those human and non-human stakeholders that are key entities in your life. Be sure to incorporate those on the periphery, or who might exert a more temporary influence (e.g., your current boss) but who nonetheless have influence in your life now.

Step 3: Uncover your world

Write a statement that summarises the significance, and influence in your life, of each person, pet and organisation.

Note what you get from the relationship, what you give to the relationship, and how you would feel and react if and when the relationship ends.

Below are a series of prompt questions for each stakeholder.

1. Why is this stakeholder in your life?
   - By choice, necessity, coincidence or routine?
   - Are they a permanent (e.g., family member) or temporary (e.g., a work supervisor) fixture in your life?
2. How do you feel about this stakeholder?
3. What needs does this stakeholder have? Which of their needs must be considered in your Life Map (e.g., schooling, care arrangements, careers)?
4. What influence do you have over this stakeholder?
   - Is it something you were aware of?
   - Is it positive or negative?
   - What risk or opportunity does this present to you and fulfilment of your Life Drivers and goals?
5. What influence does this stakeholder have over you?
   - Is it something you were aware of it?
   - Is it positive of negative?
   - What risk or opportunity does this pose to you and fulfilment of your Life Drivers and goals?

6. What routines or habits is this stakeholder involved with you in? (e.g., getting daily coffee together, or Sunday brunch, or taking the dog for a walk).

   - Does this routine contribute to your life and wellbeing?
   - Is it something to improve, reduce or continue?

7. What obstacles does this stakeholder represent?

   - Consider whether their needs conflict with your goals (e.g., you are unable to pursue a career promotion without interfering with your partner's career path; or, does your support of your young grandchildren determine where you have to live in retirement?)
   - Does this stakeholder cause you emotional or psychological turmoil, either purposefully or not?

8. What opportunities does this stakeholder provide? (e.g., does this organisation offer you career opportunity? Can your partner support and encourage your university study? Can a close friend give you emotional support? Does providing childcare to your grandchild keep you fit and active?)

Physical domain – The ocean makes me feel alive!

We are heavily influenced by the people around us; this is understood instinctively. The influence of our external physical environment is, perhaps, given less consideration, although it is becoming increasingly better known through concepts such as Feng Shui, the minimalist movement, and more generally an awareness of the rise in consumerism and the impact of clutter on stress levels. What these all have in common is the base understanding that our physical environment impacts our physical and mental wellbeing.

One of the things that I love about travel, and I particularly experienced in my 20s backpacking through Europe, was how free I felt with limited possessions. Without a home to rent, filled with furniture I had to buy and the associated costs of utilities, internet, maintenance etc., I felt physically lighter. All I had to worry about was what I was carrying in my backpack. Sometimes the burden of the physical possessions in our lives, and the costs of maintaining them, can act like a weight on your shoulders.

The impact of physical environment on behaviour and wellbeing has been extensively researched in healthcare. In an analysis of over 600 studies, Ulrich, Zimring and co-workers found that aspects of hospital design can influence clinical outcomes. Some ways these outcomes can be improved are by ensuring there are views of or exposure to nature, improved ventilation and lighting, and using design to minimise noise.

Most people have experienced living, staying or working somewhere they did not like – whether it was the layout of the house, the amount of light and air, the colour scheme, noise, or where it was located. Living somewhere unpleasant may have made you feel depressed, restless or unhealthy. You may have actively avoided spending much time there. Possible impacts may have included eating out more frequently (if you did not like the kitchen) or spending extra money to entertain yourself outside the home. You may have had an office space with no windows or natural light, or been in an open office where proximity to others and the noise made it difficult to be productive, or left you feeling drained. When we think about the places we spend the most amount of time in, it is worth considering their impact on our choices and behaviours. They may well be impacting you in ways that you are not aware of.

The smaller things in our physical domain can also act as triggers for emotions and behaviour. Does the sight of a towel on the bathroom floor immediately infuriate you? Or does driving past a particular fast-food restaurant always spark a desire to pull into the drive-through, even though you might not be hungry? By understanding how aspects of our physical domain can positively and/or negatively trigger certain feelings or behaviours, we can look at ways to manipulate our environment to support our desires. You can build positive triggers into your life and avoid negative ones. For example, if your gym is conveniently located between where you live and your workplace, so that you must drive past it, you will find it easier to incorporate regular gym attendance into your routine. If you can change your daily commute to avoid the allure of a particular fast-food restaurant, you can avoid that negative trigger. Once you appreciate how your physical environment can support or sabotage your decisions, you can take action to ensure the physical domain is working **for** you, not against you.

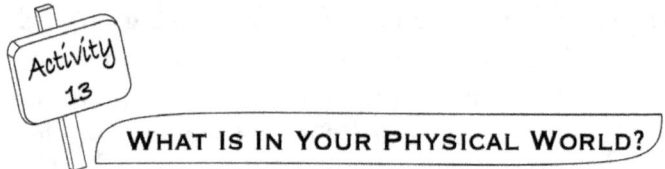

What Is In Your Physical World?

Time now to consider your physical environment.

Think about the world that you physically inhabit; write a list of all the places you reside in or visit regularly. Consider:

- Your home, especially the parts in your home that may be 'yours' more than others' (perhaps the

Step 3: Uncover your world

kitchen is your domain, or a home office, the garden or shed).

- Where you work and, specifically, your workspace.
- The suburb or town where you live and work.
- Your commute; consider both the physical route and the method of travel. Do you have your own car, take public transport, or cycle, walk etc.?
- The cafes, stores, gym, beaches, parks or other places that you frequent.

Write a summary of how often you use, and how you feel in, each space. Describe how each space influences, permits or prohibits your negative and positive habits, and whether you have control over, and the ability to change, the space. These questions are to help prompt you:

1. How much time do you spend in this space?
    - Do you have a choice about how much time you spend in this space?
2. How much control do you have over this space?
    - Are you permitted, or able, to make changes to it? (e.g., living in a rental property and not being permitted to paint the walls)
    - How much change can you make?
    - Is there a cost involved?
3. How do you feel when you are in this space?
4. What is good about this physical space?
5. What is bad about this physical space?

6. What routines or habits does this space inspire or inhibit?

    - Does this routine contribute to your life and wellbeing?

    - Are these habits or routines to improve, reduce or continue?

7. What obstacles does this space represent?

    - Consider financial aspects, such as obligations (mortgage, maintenance); time costs (maintenance, travel distances)?

    - Does this physical space cause you physical, emotional or mental discomfort?

8. What opportunities does this space provide?

    - Consider financial benefits (renting a room, building a home office).

    - Does this physical space bring you physical, emotional or psychological benefits? (Meditation space, sense of peace while drinking morning coffee/tea, encourages you to cook healthy food.)

Information domain – I saw it on the internet, so it must be true

New technologies are often criticised as bad influences. In ancient times, when oratory dominated, Socrates warned against the dangers of writing and its impact on memory, truth and wisdom. When the printing press was invented in the 15th Century, there were concerns expressed about the negative effects of mass printed books. The same happened with the telegraph, radio, and many other inventions to improve communication. All of these technologies were feared to bring laziness and distraction, and to reduce virtue in some way.

Fast forward to the 1960s when fears about the influence of television prompted decades of research into modelling of behaviour. Albert Bandura's social learning experiments with the Bobo doll showed that aggressive behaviour in children was learned by witnessing violent behaviour in adults. Children who observed an adult hit, punch and act aggressively towards the Bobo doll (a toy with a rounded bottom that has a low centre of gravity that rocks back and forth) were significantly more likely to engage in the same behaviour. This led the way for further research to see if such imitations of violence could also be observed from violent cartoons and TV shows throughout the 1970s and 80s. Since then, the effects of a range of media content, including social media, gaming and online pornography, have also been extensively researched with regard to impacts on gender stereotypes, self-esteem, sexual habits, and physical and mental health. Without a doubt, the ideas and images we are exposed to influence us in a range of ways and to varying extents.

The 21st Century information-rich environment is intricately intertwined with the potentially insidious influences of advertising, and political and agenda messaging. Although the influence of advertising has been thoroughly researched over the past 70 years, the lines between advertising, information and misinformation are becoming increasingly blurred.

Advertising is a dominant part of modern world culture. With the growth of social media, influencers, and targeted personalised advertising derived from algorithms that take into account your internet search history, it is sometimes impossible to know if something is genuinely your own idea or if you have been influenced without your realising it. These lines are blurred further because ordinary people share and promote social media posts that appeal to them, generally without fact-checking or confirming their truth and validity. Given our constant exposure to, and the prevalence of, misinformation and 'fake news', we would all be astounded to learn exactly by how much our thoughts and opinions have been shaped by the media, advertising and agenda messaging. The important thing to learn from this is that we are influenced, consciously and unconsciously, by exposure to everything we see and hear, and these influences can be both positive and negative. The key is to be aware of what you are exposing your mind to daily, and challenging your perceptions and opinions by not blindly accepting claims made by self-proclaimed experts or social media posts.

It is also essential to be aware of how much time you spend passively in front of a screen (as opposed to time spent at a computer actively working in employment or in communicating with others). If you are not sure of how much time you waste, maintain a diary for a week. 'Screen' is not just television and movies; include gaming, watching YouTube, random internet searches, and looking at social media posts. How many hours a day are you wasting?

Once you realise how much screen time you spend, assess how much of it is beneficial to you. This does not mean you should not indulge in trashy television when the mood takes you. I enjoy watching documentaries, but also find a fictional TV series or movie is exactly what is needed when I want to relax and escape into a fantasy world. It can also be fun conducting internet searches, looking up topics that strike my interest to expand my knowledge. What you want to identify is if you have fallen into a habit of television watching, internet surfing or social media scrolling with a mindlessness that wastes your time and, potentially, encourages other bad habits (mindless eating, drinking too much soda or alcohol). Do not be concerned when you find out how much time you spend passively in front of a screen; this is an opportunity to have more productive time in your day.

Activity 14: Your Ideas, Communication and hobbies

It is time to examine those aspects of the information domain that dominate your life.

Consider the following in terms of how much time and effort you devote to them, and what you would like to do but either do not do enough of, or at all (e.g., you used to play guitar but never find time for it any more).

1. **Ideas.** What type of books, websites and magazines you read, movies or YouTube channels you watch, education you are engaged in (courses, study, independent research).

2. **Communication.** Social media, gaming, other internet or virtual groups you engage with.

3. **Hobbies.** This can include a range of activities, such as gardening, crafts, music, woodworking, motorcycle riding, amateur photography… The possibilities are endless!

Write a statement summarising your ideas, communication/interactions and hobbies. How do these influence you? What negative and positive habits do they support? The following questions may help prompt you:

1. How much time do you spend on this?
   - Should you be spending more or less time on this?
   - Is this a part of your daily/weekly routine? Should it be?
2. How does this make you feel?
3. What is good about this?
4. What is bad about this?
5. What routines or habits does this activity/ idea inspire or detract?
   - Does this routine contribute to what you want to achieve in your life?
   - Does this routine contribute to to your wellbeing?
   - Is it something to improve, reduce or continue?
6. What hobbies / activities would you like to start, re-start or dedicate more time to?

Step 3 Summary

You have now finished Step 3 and, along with it, **Part I: Take Stock**. At this point you will have developed a clearer understanding of yourself, your aspirations and your environment, and the impact all these have on your thoughts, behaviours and decisions. It is incredible how much the analysis you have done will help ground you, and give you confidence in your future endeavours. If you do nothing further with this process, you will still benefit from the in-depth and objective understanding of your world that you have now developed.

Step 3: Uncover your world

I have my own Take Stock outcomes from following this process; when I am feeling conflicted, I like to read through it to remind myself that I am on the right path for me. It reminds me what is important to me, and gives me the focus I need to face challenges, make life decisions, or cope with hardships.

With your analysis complete, you are now ready to Take Control – to put this analysis into your Life Map to navigate your way forward and into the life you desire.

STEP 3 OUTCOMES

ACTIVITY 12: WHO ARE YOUR STAKEHOLDERS?
ACTIVITY 13: WHAT IS IN YOUR PHYSICAL WORLD?
ACTIVITY 14: YOUR IDEAS, COMMUNICATION AND HOBBIES

PART II
TAKE CONTROL

CHAPTER 6
STEP 4: DESIGN YOUR LIFE MAP

> *Someone's sitting in the shade today because someone planted a tree a long time ago.*
> —Warren Buffett

YOU HAVE NOW taken stock; you know where you have come from and understand what brought you here; you are clear on your current situation. You are also enlightened and percipient to your Life Drivers, your capabilities and vulnerabilities, your Life Philosophy and the external influences that affect and shape you, and the world around you. The next step is to figure out where you choose to go, not where you will go if you let life just take you, like a passenger gazing out the window as life passes by. It is time to get in the driver's seat.

STEP 4: DESIGN YOUR LIFE MAP

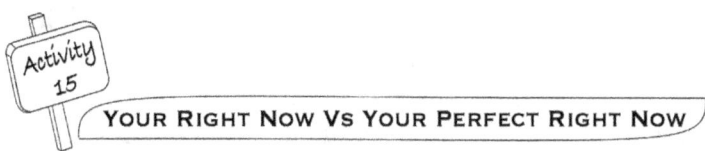

YOUR RIGHT NOW VS YOUR PERFECT RIGHT NOW

It is time to do a final review of where you are now before we move forward. Think back to Activity 1, Your Life Right Now, where you answered questions about your current situation. Okay, now let us look at the same questionnaire, but answer the questions as if, right now, you are living your perfect life (a realistic perfect, no Lotto wins or magic wish versions!).

You will note that questions 8, 9 and 10 are not included below; however, the way you answered them in Activity 1 may give you some direction for how to approach the other questions in this activity. You can also draw on all that you have discovered throughout Take Stock to inform what this perfect version should look like.

So, in your Perfect Life Right Now:

1. Where are you living?
2. Who are you living with?
3. What do you do for work, study, volunteering, hobbies etc.?
4. What is your financial situation?
5. How are you living your life? (Include routines and habits.)
6. Who is important in your life?
7. What else in your life is important to you?

Now compare the two. What differences are there? Which of these differences is now in your power to change, and what is outside of your control? As we move into the rest of this Step, this activity should facilitate building our Life Map to create the life you want to be living.

Where to from here?

In Take Stock, and in Activity 15 (above), you may have identified that you are in the right place and your life is already moving in the direction you want it to go. Moving forward, you can design your Life Plan to ensure you continue down the path you have started. Perhaps where you are now is not exactly what you want, but it is pretty close, so you want to make just some small changes. Perhaps you have looked at yourself and your life and are wondering how on earth you ended up in this place, and are determined to change direction completely. Wherever you find yourself, now is the time to Take Control. By mapping out your Life Plan, you will know where to plant the seedlings that will grow to be the trees you will need in the future.

Keep in mind when writing a Life Plan that the nearer periods of time will contain a lot more detail. It is easier to forecast and plan for tomorrow than it is to plan a day a year from now, as you have more information about what exactly is or will be happening tomorrow. If you plan a picnic for tomorrow, you will know what the weather will probably be like, have a more accurate RSVP list, have the menu ready, and so on. If planning the same picnic for next year, you will have to make some assumptions about these details, based on your understanding of what the weather is likely to be (depending on the season), and who is going to show up (determined by how well you know the invitees and their lives). However, there will be finer details that cannot be determined until closer to that future date; you may require a contingency plan for wet weather, or last-minute changes to attendees or menus.

So, as you develop your Life Map out to 10, 20, and 30 plus years, the level of detail will reduce, and the content will be broader and less specific. As you move through life, your Life Plan will act as a framework or guideposts that you can revise and refine as time passes.

The goal is to create a detailed 6 month to 2-year plan, a somewhat detailed 2- to 5-year plan, a framework 10-year plan, and then beyond that a rough outline, based on your known milestones, expectations and aspirations, and some contingencies. By coming back to your plan and reviewing it regularly, you can reassess your progress, incorporate any new goals or considerations from your world analysis, remove outdated aspects, adjust timelines, and reflect on the reasons behind any failed progress.

Milestones and goals

To get started you need to identify the known milestones and goals in your life. These will form the framework or structure for your plan and essentially act as waypoints to build your Life Map into Phases. Milestones include major events for both you and significant stakeholders in your life, and can include such things as upcoming weddings, pregnancies, graduations, buying a home and promotions. Goals can be significant things you want to achieve in your life, or personal challenges or desires you want to accomplish. Sometimes a goal and a milestone will be entwined (such as graduating from university).

Some milestones will have a definite time associated with them. These date-specific milestones include significant birthdays, education-related milestones (for yourself and your family members), career, financial and contract-based milestones.

Other milestones may have time-related windows that you can anticipate, but may happen unexpectedly, such as the passing of loved ones, changing careers, or relocating. These can include fertility-related windows, particularly if you are a woman who wants to have children one day, and the anticipated health deterioration of loved ones and pets due to age. Other time windows may be financial, such as anticipating the burden of school fees, expected promotions, or when you envisage you will have paid off your mortgage.

Finally, you may have goals or desires that do not have a time attached. These can include travel, 'bucket list' aspirations (e.g., completing a marathon, writing a book, learning to play an instrument), or may include things like buying your first home, or career goals that you want to work towards without a specific time frame attached. These are referred to as flexible goals.

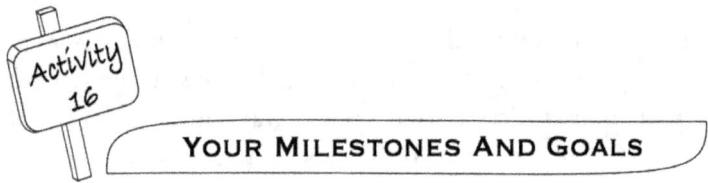

YOUR MILESTONES AND GOALS

Look at the categories listed below and consider the time-specific, time-window and flexible-specific milestones and goals for your life.

Look back over activities you have completed for inspiration and guidance, as in some instances you will have already

Step 4: Design your Life Map

identified a number of milestones and goals. For example, when looking at Step 1, were there any patterns in your thoughts or behaviour you were looking to change? From Step 2, is there something you learned from your vulnerabilities or Life Philosophy that has inspired a goal? In Step 3, is there anything you uncovered from analysis of your stakeholders, physical or information domains that you would like to develop in to a milestone or goal? Also consider what you have uncovered when comparing your life right now to what your perfect life would look like – what was missing? What changes can you make, goals can you identify that will help you shift the course of your life so that it is more aligned with the life you want to have.

Once you have made your list, using a highlighter or different-coloured pens, distinguish between those milestones that are time-specific, time-window or flexible.

	MILESTONES	GOALS
CAREER		
EDUCATION		
FAMILY		
FRIENDS		
HOME		
HEALTH		
FITNESS		
FINANCIAL		
TRAVEL		
HOBBIES		
SPIRITUAL		
PERSONAL DEVELOPMENT		

Timeline design

Once you have your list, you are ready to design a timeline. Your timeline could be framed by calendar year (1st January to 31st December), by your birthday, or other significant annual event. For me, it was relatively easy to decide; being born in January and living in Australia, the natural frame for me is the

Step 4: Design your Life Map

calendar year. January marks the beginning of a New Year for me in every sense, and when combined with the summer and Christmas holiday period, usually provides some down-time for self-reflection.

Once you decide on the frame for your timeline, you then need to break it down into different-sized chunks – shorter and more detailed phases at the start, and larger phases further down the time-track. You may want to get creative with the chunks of time and consider naming the phases. Here is an example:

Phase 1: Getting it together

    a. 2025: Monthly / Quarterly

    b. 2026: January – June

    c. 2026: July – December

Phase 2: Hitting my stride

    2027: 12-month block

Phase 3: Final countdown (kids finishing school)

    2028 to 2029: 2-year block

Phase 4: Empty nesting

    2030 to 2034: 5-year block

Phase 5: The Middle Ages

    2035 to 2044: 10-year block

Phase 6: Twilight years

    2045 to 2064: 20-year block

This framework will set your Life Map. As each year ends, you can look back over the past 12 months to see what things worked according to plan and what curveballs you may have managed. You will then be able to review and update your next phase so that you always have a more detailed plan for your next 12 months, with subsequent blocks reduced in size. So, you will have a constantly evolving timeline where your next 12 to 24 months are updated and refined with greater detail.

Using the above example, as 2026 commences this is how the plan could change with more detail for Phase 1 and 2. Continuing the example below, for Phase 1, the first half of 2026 will have detailed monthly plans, with the second half of the year split into three-month blocks. For Phase 2, the year has been split into six-monthly time periods.

Phase 1: Getting it together

    a. 2026: Monthly

    b. 2026: July – September

    c. 2026: October - December

Phase 2: Hitting my stride

    a. 2027: January–June

    b. 2027: July–December

STEP 4: DESIGN YOUR LIFE MAP

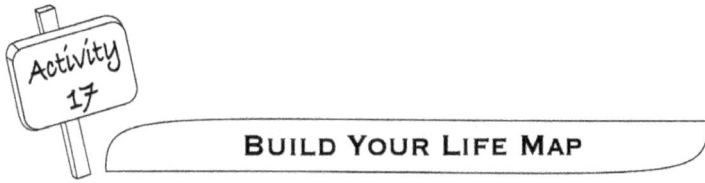

BUILD YOUR LIFE MAP

It is time to build your Life Map! There is an example later in this chapter and a template can be found in the appendices at the end of this book or at TakeCommandLifePlanning.com. As always, do not feel constrained by format and create your own template if you are inspired to do so.

Design your timeline by deciding what periods of time your Phases will consist of.

Once you have your timeline, look over your milestones and goals and simply insert them at the appropriate place. Starting with those that are time-based, you can then look to insert other goals where they will best fit. For example, it is probably not a good idea to plan for that epic overseas holiday the same year you expect to buy your first home.

You should also consider major events that you have not included as a milestone or a goal. You best friend's upcoming wedding, or a family holiday might not yet be captured; however, it is a significant event that you want to include in your Life Map. Such events possibly require planning or budgeting which may need to be a consideration in the lead-up to their occurrence.

Once you have framed your Life Map with your goals, milestones and events, look at where you need to start certain daily habits or activities in preparation for achieving your goals and reaching milestones, and include them. If you have a goal for achieving a certain grade for your study at the end of the year, this is the time to ensure you have set the bite-sized goals and habits along the way that will get you there. If you want to make a career change, can you act immediately, or do you need to devise a longer-term strategy to gain new qualifications, or develop your professional network? If your 50th birthday is a milestone, and you want to have a particular celebration for it, how far out do you plan for it? If it is to be a large party, do you need to start a year beforehand to set aside a small amount of money each payday? If your milestone is attached to a goal, such as going skydiving for the first time, is there something you need to do earlier to make sure that it happens? The whole point is that, when the time comes for you to achieve that goal or reach that milestone, you have what you need and are prepared.

This is also the point at which you should make sure you are including outputs from Step 3 in your Life Map that you did not identify as a milestone or a goal. Do you need to include on your Life Map anything regarding your stakeholders – such as your wife's anticipated promotion, or your ageing dog needing expensive medical care? Was there anything you became aware of from your physical environment that you want to include, such as incorporating a weekly visit to a park or the ocean, personalising your workspace, decluttering your home, planning a renovation or creating a herb garden? And from your information environment: are you planning to restrict the amount of time you spend watching television or using social media? Will you start a daily journal, resume learning karate, or finally learn to play the piano?

When building these ideas into your Life Map, be sure not to start everything all at once! Although you may decide to start journaling immediately, you can build your vegetable garden in the spring, and train to run a marathon next year (or the year after!). If you overwhelm yourself with immediate goals

Step 4: Design your Life Map

and habits or hobbies, you will achieve nothing. Building a Life Map is not about doing everything all at once; it is about understanding yourself, your current priorities and drivers, and what makes you happy. A Life Map is for ensuring that you take the time throughout your life to fill it with joy and personal challenges. You can always bring forward or delay a goal, hobby or habit if need be. Remember, life is not a race, it is a journey, and not one that you want to rush.

Some final words of advice: look at your plan and make sure you are achieving balance in all aspects of your life. Are you focusing solely on your career to the detriment of everything else? Are you trying to do too much, not leaving yourself any time for relaxation and personal care? And does your Life Map resonate with your Life Philosophy? Do you feel good about the plan you are developing? Actually creating and documenting your Life Plan gives you the opportunity to ensure you are taking care of your life in its entirety and staying true to who you are and what you want your life to be.

Where are your Life Drivers?

Remember identifying your Life Drivers in Step 2? It is now time to look over your Life Map and make sure you are addressing each of your Life Drivers over the course of your life. Try to identify which drivers are the priority for you in different phases. While you have children at home, it is likely that the dominant driver will be family-centric; or perhaps, after you have started your family, career or financial drivers become important? At different times in your life, different things will take priority and you may need to choose one driver over another, even if only temporarily. Knowing what is most important to you at different times in your life will help you make decisions that enhance your life's journey. This will help give you the strength and conviction to act in a way that is true to yourself and what is best for you and your loved ones. For example, do you turn down a job opportunity that would be detrimental to your family's best interests, or act at the right time to take a risk in business, or to pack up your worldly belongings and hit the road. Knowing which drivers are important to you in your different life stages will help you know what action you need to take to achieve and maintain the life you want.

It is important for your personal fulfilment that you ensure each of your Life Drivers is incorporated into your Life Map during at least one phase. If any one of them is not put in the Life Map, then you must ask whether it is a driver after all. Perhaps it is a goal rather than a Life Driver. Or are you disregarding a Life Driver permanently, by failing to address it, and possibly leading to dissatisfaction in life? You do not want to be going through a midlife crisis at age 45 because you feel you have not yet addressed one of your Life Drivers; or in old age, lying on your deathbed with regret. The difference between a goal and a Life Driver is that you can generally reconcile not following through on a goal. If you move through your life without finding a way to satisfy each of your Life Drivers, you will feel like you have not fulfilled your life's purpose. Find a way to satisfy each of your Life Drivers throughout the course of your life and you will find contentment.

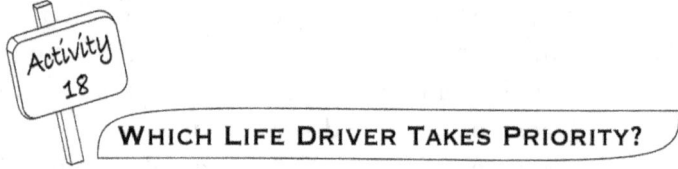

Activity 18

WHICH LIFE DRIVER TAKES PRIORITY?

Review your Life Map and consider which of your Life Drivers will be the priority for each phase. You may have more than one as a priority, or you may not be able to identify what your priority Life Driver will be for later phases. As a minimum, ensure the phase you are in now has a priority identified.

Life Map example

Let's look at a fictional example Life Map. Here we have Angela, who is married with a young son and is pregnant with her second child (a daughter). Again, like the example for the Phase 0 Life Map, as a fictional example there is less detail than you will likely have in your Life Map. For example, in Phase 1a you will see that Angela has a goal to have everything ready for the baby's arrival; if this was your own Life Map you would list everything you wanted to have completed, rather than make a general overarching statement.

You will also note that goals, milestones and major events are noted, along with which Life Drivers are the priority for Angela in each phase.

Angela's Life Map

Phase 1a.	2021: Preparing for baby	Priority Driver/s
September to December	<ul><li>Keep up exercise routine (gym twice a week and daily walks). Reduce intensity as needed in later pregnancy.</li><li>Keep putting money each pay into Maternity Leave fund.</li><li>**October**: Plan romantic weekend. Organise for my sister to look after my son (**EVENT**).</li><li>**24 December:** Have everything ready for the baby's arrival (**GOAL**).</li><li>Christmas at my parents' house (**EVENT**).</li></ul>	Family (1) Health and fitness (3)

Phase 1b	2022: Settling new baby and return to fitness	Priority Driver/s
January to June	<ul><li>Keep up exercise routine as long as possible before birth (gym twice a week and daily walks). Reduce intensity as needed.</li><li>Last day of work 15 January – start Maternity Leave.</li><li>Start new budget.</li><li>**February** Baby due (**MILESTONE**).</li><li>**April**: Return to regular exercise routine (**GOAL**).</li></ul>	Family (1) Health and fitness (3)
July to December	<ul><li>Exercise routine back to pre-pregnancy.</li><li>Maintain budget.</li><li>**September / October**: Plan for family beach holiday (**EVENT**).</li></ul>	

Phase 2	2023 – 2025: Getting back to work	Priority Driver/s
2023	<ul><li>**February:** I return to work part time.</li><li>**May:** I return to work full time.</li><li>Plan a South Pacific cruise for end of the year (**GOAL**).</li><li>**December:** Dad is due to retire (**MILESTONE**).</li></ul>	Family (1)
2024	<ul><li>Renovate main bathroom and kitchen (**GOAL**).</li><li>**February:** Son starts school (**MILESTONE**).</li><li>**November 2024:** Husband's 40th birthday (**MILESTONE**).</li></ul>	Family (1)

In the segment below, you will note that Angela has a goal to run a marathon before she turns 40. While for the moment it is noted in her Life Map, when the time is approaching and she is updating her plan, that will be the opportunity to put in more detail to prepare for the run. Four to six months before the actual event, she can include a running program as a part of her Life Map.

Step 4: Design your Life Map

Phase 3	2025 – 2030: Supporting Husband's career and kids' schooling	Priority Driver/s
2025 - 2027	• Husband due for promotion in this time period.	Family (1)
2025	• Complete a marathon before my birthday (**GOAL**). • October 2025: My 40th birthday (**MILESTONE**).	Adventure (2)
2026	• February 2026: Daughter starts school (**MILESTONE**). • Start to develop my online business (**GOAL**). • Plan a trip to Japan.	
2027	• Dog will be 12 years old (health may start to deteriorate). • Plan a trip to New Zealand (**GOAL**).	
2028 - 2030	• Online business is successful, and I am able to leave my day job (**GOAL**).	

At this point, Angela starts to make her Life Map more general in nature. She now just highlights the goals, milestones and events that she expects will be notable during each phase.

Phase 4	2030 – 2040: Focus on kids' education and getting out of debt	Priority Driver/s
MILESTONES: **February 2031:** Son starts high school. **February 2033:** Daughter starts high school. **November 2034:** Husband's 50th birthday. **October 2035:** My 50th birthday. **November 2036:** Son graduates high school. **November 2038:** Daughter graduates from high school. **GOALS:** **2038 - 2040:** Mortgage paid in full / no more debt. **EVENTS:** **2034-2035:** Plan a family trip to Italy & Spain.		Family (1) Adventure (2)

Phase 5	2040 + (20 years and beyond): Enjoying retirement	Priority Driver/s
2065 – 2070: • **MILSTONE**: Both my husband and I retire. • **GOAL**: Travel around Australia. • **GOAL**: Learn to play guitar. 2070 – 2075: • **GOAL**: Downsize and move to smaller house, ideally close to children and any grandchildren.		Adventure (2) Health (3)

Step 4 Summary

We have reached the end of Step 4, and you now have a Life Map! It has been a lot of work to get to this point, and we are on the home stretch now. Moving into Step 5, you will discover how to refine your Life Map and come up with some strategies to prepare for those curveballs that life is going to throw your way.

STEP 4 OUTCOMES

ACTIVITY 15: YOUR RIGHT NOW VS YOUR PERFECT RIGHT NOW
ACTIVITY 16: YOUR MILESTONES AND GOALS
ACTIVITY 17: BUILD YOUR LIFE MAP
ACTIVITY 18: WHICH LIFE DRIVER TAKES PRIORITY?

CHAPTER 7
STEP 5: ENHANCE YOUR LIFE MAP

Plan for what is difficult while it is easy.
—Sun Tzu

OKAY, SO NOW you have a plan! Your very own Life Map. However, at this point your plan is almost certainly biased towards the positive, based on things working out the way that you hope they will. But things rarely turn out exactly the way we hope; Fate, circumstance, or straight up bad luck is unavoidable. When things go wrong it can be difficult to see clearly and objectively in that moment as the initial reaction and emotional response can cloud rational thinking. Following Sun Tzu's guidance, the best time to plan for the bad is when life is good and you can prepare physically, mentally and emotionally.

Step 5: Enhance your Life Map

Over the past few decades, the positive psychology movement has dominated the narrative. This concept proposes that positive thinking and visualisation will allow you to manifest your aspirations and that even contemplating failure will make failing inevitable. Creating vision boards, repeating positive affirmations, suppressing self-doubt and ignoring criticism was the way to bring you whatever you desire, such as fame, riches, the perfect body or partner. Although such tools can support success, simply daydreaming and wishing for a perfect life is not a means to achieve it.

When you let yourself contemplate the negative, you are increasing your likelihood of success. In identifying and understanding the risks to your plan, to achieving a goal, you can gain power over it. If you know what could go wrong, you can develop ways to overcome the obstacle and improve the chance of things going your way. If you only ever focus on the positive, on things happening in an idealised scenario, you will be underprepared for when things do go wrong. If an engaged couple consider what might arise in their lives that could cause marital problems, then they can come up with strategies to overcome those issues should they arrive. This is essentially what can be achieved through pre-marriage counselling, which is simply leveraging an objective professional who can provide advice on techniques such as effective communication. If the Olympic champion has considered that risks to her success include bad weather or extreme heat, she can prepare for it.

The refusal to consider negative outcomes can also reduce resilience and compound disappointment when, despite focusing only on the positive, an individual is faced with a negative outcome. If you have not contemplated the possibility of not obtaining a gold medal, when you win a silver medal instead you will be disproportionally upset and emotionally unprepared to deal with the loss. An Olympic competitor may break a world record;

however, he might be in a race where the guy next to him also beats the world record and comes first in the process. Instead of celebrating winning silver and achieving a personal, and world record breaking best, he may be fixated on the fact he did not come first and win the gold medal. There is nothing he could do; he has performed at his best but in the end someone else was the better on race day. No doubt the many tantrums and sore losers observed in sporting events is indicative of failure to accept the possibility and prepare for not achieving first place.

In recent years, acknowledgment that oppressive positivity can be detrimental has increased. Forcing positivity can make it difficult for people to openly discuss their true feelings and fears, or even address those feelings internally. It is okay for someone diagnosed with cancer to contemplate a failure of their treatment; this does not mean they are welcoming death. It simply means they are processing their emotions and preparing themselves for what could go wrong. Contemplating things going wrong will not send an invitation to the Universe to manifest a negative outcome. In fact, it is the smartest thing you can do to improve your chances of success and build resilience. Someone can be optimistic and focused a positive outcome and yet still take the time to contemplate the worst that could happen.

The take-away message here is not that being positive is a bad thing, the important point is striking a balance between positive thinking and negative contemplation. Incorporating both is essential for good mental health and to maximise your potential.

In Step 5 you are contemplating the negative. You are looking at what could go wrong, so that you can avoid it where possible or, if not, come through it with resilience. I call this process Life-gaming. By understanding the risk, and identifying and developing Divergent Point path options for your future self,

Step 5: Enhance your Life Map

you fortify yourself with pre-prepared choices that you can refer to when required.

For some people, contemplating failure to achieve their goals is a difficult task. However, if you do not consider the possibility of failure then, should the worst happen, you will be emotionally unprepared to deal with the reality of it. Preparing for failure is not about giving up, or not doing your best to achieve a goal, it is about hoping for the best, and doing everything in your power to succeed, but also contemplating and preparing yourself to cope and adjust if the worst does happen. Keep in mind, sometimes the plan for failure to attain a goal is to try, try and try again! As the famous Japanese martial artist Morihei Ueshiba once said, 'Failure is the key to success; each mistake teaches us something.' I implore you to contemplate failure the same as you do success, and see the opportunities presented whatever may occur.

What is Life-gaming?

Life-gaming is essentially contemplating how risks, obstacles, or opportunities might impact your plans. When you conduct a life-game, you develop 'what if' scenarios. The process works by assessing the risks to your preferred plan, imagining possible scenarios of what could happen, and challenging what you expect or want to happen. You then examine what options may be available to you should you reach a Divergent Point and Life-game some alternate paths. The process is summarised in this flow chart:

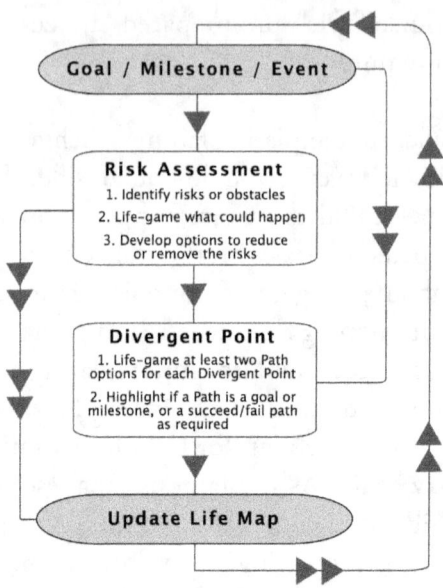

So, in this step, you will conduct a risk assessment on significant goals, milestones or events contained within your Life Map, and strengthen your plan against these risks. You then consider if success or failure of the goal/milestone/event could place you on a Divergent Point. A Divergent Point is essentially that fork in the road, where the road diverges into multiple paths that you may have to choose between. As a part of this process, you will then develop scenarios to test your plan and develop the path options you will have available to you. Perhaps one path becomes blocked if you do not achieve a certain goal (a success/fail path), or you have multiple paths that you must choose between due to success.

Risk Assessment

Risk assessment in a critical part of the business world and throughout government departments. Often used in the context of workplace health and safety, it is also applied to security

Step 5: Enhance your Life Map

and financial risk analysis and can be used by individuals (especially for personal investments), as well as organisations (insurance companies, banks, businesses, governments).

In doing a risk assessment of your Life Map, you are essentially looking for ways to improve your plan. Finding out what the risks are to your plan unfolding the way you want it to, and understanding how they could impact your success. Once you know what they are, you have the opportunity to neutralise or mitigate the risks to improve your chance of success. It is a practical way to incorporate worthwhile changes and protect yourself against failure.

This is a game of 'what if' in which you imagine possible scenarios where you could face obstacles to your aspirations, and come up with solutions to these anticipated obstacles. Although it is impossible to predict every possible setback, by considering the impact of potential obstacles, you will also become more adept at problem solving more generally. This will enhance your capacity to deal with both those scenarios you have anticipated as well as unexpected problems that may arise.

After examining your risks, you should identify ways to reinforce your plan with solutions to reduce or remove the risk. For example, do you look at increasing your contribution to your house deposit savings if you think there could be an interest rate rise, or housing boom? Can you improve your ability to achieve the grade you need by hiring a tutor? Will your dating prospects improve if you expand your social circle? Here you are enhancing your plan so that it has a greater possibility of working the way you want it to.

After doing your risk assessment, you will probably identify some Divergent Points. Divergent Points may be triggered by either the success or failure to reach a goal or milestone, or when an event occurs that requires a decision. Whatever the reason behind it, whether due to a success, failure or other event outcome, a Divergent Point will be an opportunity.

Divergent Points

Identifying possible Divergent Points allows you to consider how a future fork in the road can send you along different paths. You may have identified the Divergent Point when doing your risk assessment; however, there may be obvious Divergent Points in your Life Map that you can consider without the need to do a risk assessment.

Everyone considers the different paths available to them at different times throughout their lives. When a high school graduate is considering what degree to study, they will contemplate how each decision could lead them down a completely different path. When someone is offered a job opportunity interstate, forcing them into a long-distance relationship, they need to decide if the job is worth the risk of possible relationship breakdown. All we are doing in this process is forecasting some likely Divergent Points at the earliest opportunity before they are imminent. You do not need to make a decision immediately; you are just putting some thought into future scenarios while you have the luxury of time and absence of pressure.

Divergent Points may be tied to milestones, so that reaching a certain milestone has the potential to send you down multiple different paths. For example, does reaching a certain career milestone lead to a Divergent Point which would require you to relocate to accept a promotion? If you are not married or in a relationship by a certain age, will you look at options to become a solo parent through donor programs? Would the passing of your elderly mother be a trigger for you to increase care for your father, potentially requiring him to live with you? Or if your daughter who lives interstate has a child, would that prompt a decision for you to sell your house to move closer to her and your grandchild?

The same process works for the achievement of or failure to reach goals. Although we often contemplate these occurrences in the abstract, it is usually only when they loom in our not-too-distant future that they grab our attention. Rather than assuming they will have the luxury of choosing between each of their preferences, the high school graduate should take time to contemplate not achieving the mark they need for acceptance into any of their preferred degree courses. In this way, they will have already devised alternative options before they are caught up in the disappointment of the moment. On the other hand, sometimes success brings too many opportunities, which can make decision making difficult. If the high school graduate achieves an unanticipated high mark, they may be overwhelmed by all the offers they receive, and feel paralysed and unable to choose from among the many options. Consider the protégé who obtains an Olympic gold medal as a teenager; how do they move forward? Do they set new goals to continue to achieve at the same level in the same sport? Or now that they have reached the pinnacle of achievement in one sport, do they look to other goals in other fields?

Before you launch in and try Life-gaming yourself, let's look at a couple of examples. In the first example our protagonist is stepping through the entire process – from risk assessment to Divergent Point analysis and the development of path options. In the second example, our protagonist is developing path options for the Divergent Points he identified in his Life Map that could arise at a career milestone.

Life-game examples

In our first example, we have a 33-year-old woman named Emma, who has recently ended her long-term relationship because of her partner's infidelity. In following the Take Command process, she has identified having children is a priority for her, and therefore is tied to the Life Driver of meeting her 'Mr Right' and having a family. Having had her life path change unexpectedly by becoming single, she has set a goal to become a mother before she is 38 years of age. Her gold standard would be to meet someone and have time to build their relationship and get married prior to starting a family. However, if this does not happen, she wants to Life-game her options. Here is her risk assessment:

Goal – Have a child by the time I am 38 years old		
Risks	**What could happen?**	**Options to treat the risk**
Not being in a relationship	I will act on my decision to become a solo parent if still single at age 38.	Ensure I am dating and meeting new people; try internet dating, join a local social club, request friends to set me up, accept blind dates, be open to meeting new people.
Being in a relationship with someone who does not want children	Possible Divergent Point. End relationship or give up on goal of being a parent.	No treatment option. This is an obstacle to my primary goal. Clear Divergent Point.
Being in a relationship with someone who cannot have children	Possible Divergent Point. Is my partner open to alternatives, such as donor sperm or adoption? Or do I end the relationship?	Path options will depend on my partner and our circumstances. I will need to consider this in depth if it occurs, as there are too many variables for a fictional scenario.
I have fertility issues	Divergent Point. Decision to pursue fertility treatment options or not.	Look at getting health insurance in advance of trying to fall pregnant so that I have financial capacity to follow through with any fertility treatments.

Step 5: Enhance your Life Map

Emma builds her treatments into her Life Map; firstly, adding goals to set up an internet dating profile and joining a local mixed soccer team. If after six months she is still having difficulty meeting a partner, she will begin to speak to her friends about setting her up with single men they know. She also looks at health insurance plans and which companies offer the best fertility treatment options and adds to her Life Map that she will get insurance by age 37. She confirms that she has made the decision that should she reach 37 years of age without a partner she will pursue becoming a solo parent. Looking at her risk assessment, she decides there are two Divergent Points that she can develop into options: Fertility issues (either with or without a partner), and Complications with a Partner. In the examples below I have used different templates to demonstrate alternative formats that can be employed in developing Divergent Points.

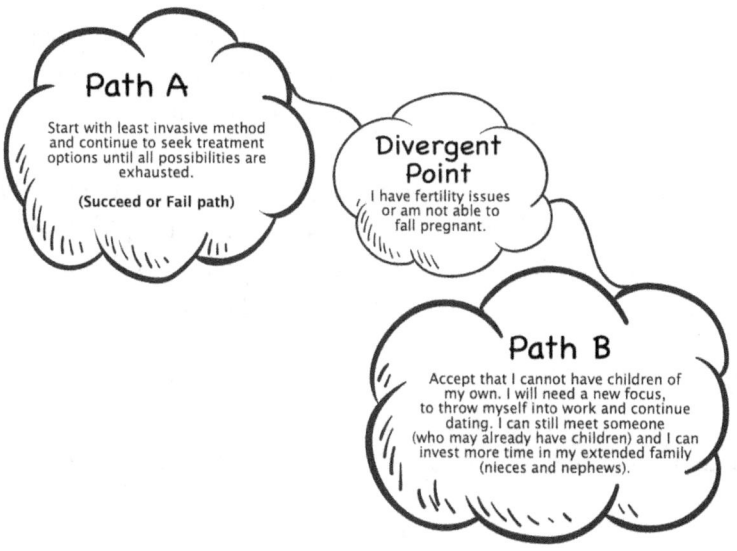

Divergent Point 2: Complications with a partner

- Path A: He does not want kids.

    I am not compromising on this. I will end the relationship. Relationships have consistently failed me to this point, and I will not give up for a partner my determination to have a child. **(Dead end path)**

- Path B: We meet when I am almost 37 and about to commence solo parenting.

    If I meet someone and he wants to have kids, but I am almost at my target age, we cannot rush into it. I will have to consider delaying trying for a baby, but I will put a timeline on how long I am prepared or able to delay, depending on my fertility.

- Path C: He wants kids, but he has fertility issues.

    This will have to be worked through with my partner at the time. This will become a joint decision on using donor sperm or looking at other options.

You will note that for Divergent Point 1, it is possible that at some point Path A will either be successful or not. If, despite all her best efforts, it is determined that Emma is infertile, this path will no longer be viable, and she will be forced onto Path B. While she could look at adopting or fostering children, she has decided this is not a path she wants to develop. Thus, if Path A does not work, or she cannot continue to attempt all available options to become a parent, she will have to take Path B.

Path A on Divergent Pint 2 is a dead end; if she meets someone who does not want to have children, she will end the relationship. Instead of being caught in the emotion of the moment, she will focus on what is most important to her;

Step 5: Enhance your Life Map

being a parent, even if it means doing it alone. For Path C on Divergent Point 2, there is not much Emma can plan for. Although she has considered this path as a possibility, what her options are and what she chooses to do will be very much dependent on the specific circumstances. For now, she has just highlighted the fact that while she may meet 'Mr Right', there may still be obstacles to overcome in having the family she desires.

In the second example, our protagonist is John, a 30-year-old married man who has two young children. He is five years into his career and has identified that reaching a career milestone of 10 years with the same company will trigger the decision to either continue in his current role and career, or to make a change. In this example, John has skipped the risk assessment, as he has already identified this milestone will trigger two possible Divergent Points.

Divergent Point 1: Promotion offered by 10-year milestone

- Path A: Accept promotion to replace current supervisor **(goal)**.

- Path B: An alternative promotion path could require a move to head office, which means an increased commute or relocation.

    I will consider this, but when the time comes, will need to assess family circumstances – will a relocation disrupt children's schooling, or my wife's employment? I may be able to negotiate to work remotely, or from home, a few days a week.

    Reasons to decline: pay increase is not sufficient compensation for additional responsibilities and hours; new supervisor is not family friendly; an unforeseen circumstance with family.

Divergent Point 2: Promotion not offered by 10-year milestone

- Path A: Continue in current position

  If I am enjoying the work, and am happy with renumeration and workplace environment, I may stay on in my current position. I will need to talk to my supervisor about my future prospects and whether promotion will ever be an option. I may be willing to work up to another five years in my current role, but after that would definitely be ready for new challenges as kids will have finished school.

- Path B: Start looking for a new job.

  Unless promotion is likely to be offered within 12 months, I will start actively looking for alternative employment in a similar field.

- Path C: Consider complete change in career.

  Rather than looking for a new job in the same field, I will commit to study part time and stay in my current role until qualified and able to change careers.

John has examined a range of possible paths and given his future self ideas to contemplate and pros and cons to consider. In this instance, although an offer of promotion is expected to occur at a particular time, by developing Divergent Point 1, he has already prepared considerations if he is offered an alternative promotion prior to his 10-year milestone. If this occurs, rather than just gleefully accepting, he has put some thought behind what it would mean for him and his family, which will aid in his decision-making process.

As you can see, the above examples leave a variety of possibilities open, and explore potential future scenarios that Emma

STEP 5: ENHANCE YOUR LIFE MAP

and John can draw on when the time comes. You also can do this for considering future health issues (such as when to have non-urgent surgery); financial windfalls or obstacles; when you can retire from the workforce; or how long you are prepared to wait before undertaking a long-held dream to travel to Antarctica or hike through the Himalayas.

Also, as you get closer to when the Divergent Point is expected to occur (for those that are time-based and can be anticipated) you can revise your options with increased detail and clarity.

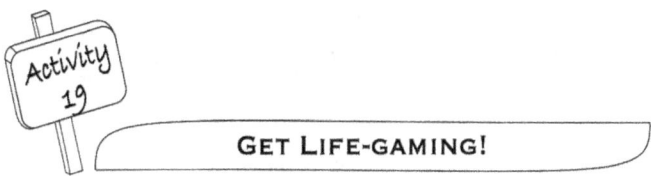

GET LIFE-GAMING!

Time to try Life-gaming, using the flow chart as a guide. There are several templates included in the appendices at the back of this book or can be found at TakeCommandLifePlanning.com. You may also be inspired to design your own format.

1. First you need to decide what goals, milestones or other events you would like to test; look at your Life Map and identify those critical moments you have planned for that have risks or potential obstacles that could hinder attainment. Decide if you want to conduct a risk assessment, to better appreciate the possible setbacks, or if you can see obvious Divergent Points arising from either a success or failure.

2. Conduct a risk assessment on your selected goals, milestones or events. You can use the template provided at the back of this book, or at TakeCommandLifePlanning.com, or use your own.

Once you have completed your risk assessment be sure to update your plan with the strategies you have identified that will either reduce or remove the risks you have identified. Where appropriate, identify Divergent Points for the development of path options.

3. Identify the Divergent Points you want to life game. These can be drawn from your risk assessment or directly from your Life Map.

4. Develop your path options for each Divergent Point. There are some templates at the back of this book, or at TakeCommandLifePlanning.com, or you can develop your own.

There is no particular way to develop your path options; it is a matter of being creative and attempting to identify the different outcomes that could arise. You can use visualisation to help imagine what might occur, you could try a mind map, or simply just writing down the scenarios in a list. Each Divergent Point should have at least two path options available. If there is only one path, then it is not a Divergent Point! If you have too many path options for a particular Divergent Point (more than five), then take a closer look at it; in most instances you should have only between two and four path options.

You do not need to spend copious amounts of time developing out countless scenarios for every moment of your life; just take those goals and milestones that have greatest importance to you and your family. Remember, you can keep coming back and adding to or revising these scenarios as new information comes

Step 5: Enhance your Life Map

to light, or as you identify more milestones or goals that may have Divergent Points.

Step 5 Summary

That is Step 5 complete, and with it, Part II: Take Control. Hopefully, you have taken the time to identify and contemplate possible future Divergent Points in your life, and how you might navigate potential obstacles. Practising this step should also provide you with some tools to apply when you are facing a decision you have not pre-prepared for, whether that be an unexpected promotion or pregnancy, or the diagnosis of an illness, or loss of income. Do not be afraid of failure, and do not be afraid to consider your options in preparation for not attaining your goals. You will experience more gratitude when you are successful if you have seriously contemplated failure; or, should the worst happen, you will have already prepared ways to cope and to manage the situation.

We now move on to Part III: Take Command, which is made up of the final step. It is here we start to live our plan and implement a method to update and revise our Life Map to remain flexible to the changing winds on our life journey.

> **Step 5 Outcomes**
> Activity 19: Get Life-gaming!

PART III
TAKE COMMAND

CHAPTER 8
STEP 6: TAKE COMMAND

What you are is what you have been. What you will be is what you do now.
—Buddha

AND HERE YOU are – the final step. However, as you now realise, this is an ongoing process and this final step is really just about putting your plan into action, and knowing when to circle back, re-evaluate and update your plan.

Making your plan work requires you to actually act on your plan. To live your life and have your Life Map to guide you. This means implementing routines and habits that will support the goals and milestones identified in your Life Map, and using the work you have completed through this process to regularly remind yourself of what is most important to you and the life you choose to lead.

Implement routines and habits

It is the things you do every day that will determine your life, and even your identity. Run every day and you become a runner; smoke every day and you become a smoker. A criticism of goal lists and longer-term planning is that they can become aspirational. If your goal is to lose 20 kg, but you do not make a plan and practise daily habits that support weight loss, then you will never lose the weight. Further, even if you do manage to lose weight in the short term by completing an 8-week challenge or restrictive diet, you will not maintain the weight loss if you revert to those past daily routines and habits that caused the weight gain in the first place (hello yoyo dieting!). Perhaps you are a police officer who wants to be a forensic psychologist; if you do not set aside the time to research what it takes to reskill, and then make the time to gain the required qualifications, you will almost certainly still be a police officer 20 years later.

To have the life you want, you need to ensure your habits and routines are implemented. You included these in your Life Plan in Step 4; now is the time to ensure you act on those habits and build them into your routine in a realistic way.

Remember your Life Drivers and your Life Philosophy

Remind yourself what is important to you: this includes both your Life Drivers and your Life Philosophy. Living in accordance with your Life Philosophy will help you stay on the path that will bring you the greatest contentment, and understanding your Life Drivers is central to making decisions that will enhance your overall satisfaction and happiness.

You are presented with many opportunities and decisions in your life; being attuned to your drivers will ensure you are staying true to yourself. It is really difficult to say no to a promotion or job opportunity, but sometimes saying no is the best decision for you and your life as a whole. Saying yes to something that will progress your career, but in a direction that is not what you want, could bring you 'success', but at a cost to you.

If you do not remind yourself of your Life Philosophy and Life Drivers every now and then, it is easy to get caught up in other people's vision. This is why the analysis of your world is also critical to your Life Map and should not be overlooked. If your partner's vision of getting married and settling down in suburbia with 2.5 kids contradicts your drive to live a life of adventure and travel, you need to be honest with yourself and them. If you are not, and you cannot achieve a compromise, you will either end up miserable or causing misery to others when you decide to walk away from your family to hike through South America in an attempt to satisfy a supressed Life Driver during a midlife crisis.

LIVE WITH YOUR LIFE MAP TO GUIDE YOU

Time to get on with it!

1. Make sure you have not committed to doing too much, too soon. If the first six months of your Life Map is bursting at the seams with new hobbies and habits, you are setting yourself up for failure. Choose just one or two things that you want to start working

on; focus on making them part of your daily/weekly routine. If you do have an ambitious goal that is your absolute priority, then let a few other things slide for the moment.

2. Take action. Turn that statement of 'take a walk every day' into action. Give yourself a minimum standard (e.g., 10-minute walk) and a gold standard (45-minute walk). Also, aim to carry out the action at the same time, on the same day. The more this pattern is repeated, the more likely it is to simply become what you do, without requiring much thought or effort. Once this happens, you have established a routine.

3. Keep a copy of your Life Drivers and Life Philosophy somewhere you can remind yourself of them when needed. Perhaps a list in your phone, or in a journal, or a notebook beside your bed. Whenever you feel a little lost, off track or just need a boost, having a copy of these readily available makes it easy to remind yourself of what is most important will keep you going and keep you on track.

4. Monitor your progress. Depending on how much you are trying to achieve, work out how frequently you need to track how you are progressing on your plan. Ideally, you do not want to be in a position where you need to refer to your Life Map constantly; you want to focus on living your life not maintaining a plan! If you have focused on identifying a handful of priorities for each month/quarter that are easy to remember and incorporate into your life you should be able to get on with living and just refer to your plan when needed.

Review and update

Your life is a journey through uncharted territory, so a Life Map is just a plan that is correct as at the moment you write it. As rough weather, good fortune or new pathways present themselves, you cannot always stick rigidly to the course you have plotted. Choose a time of year for reflection and re-evaluation of your life; revisit your Life Map annually, unless triggered by a significant event requiring immediate review, especially in the case of a Step 7 Black Swan event (which we will discuss shortly).

You need to set aside some time to update your Life Map as you move through your life. By taking this time at least once each year, you will remind yourself of your path, reinvest in yourself, and ensure you are in command of your life, living every day to support the life you want. It gives you that time to pause and reflect on the year that has just passed, as you consider what you had set out to do compared with how it actually did unfold. It also provides the opportunity to refine the details for your next phase.

It is not just your external world that can change – you may find your strengths and weaknesses, beliefs, goals or life philosophy shift in a different direction as you grow older; you will then need to re-evaluate who you are – compared to who you used to be. This can often happen when someone becomes a parent, whether planned or not. The arrival of a child has a way of changing people's priorities and even their outlook on life.

The work you have done on your Life Plan can also help when you are facing an obstacle, or even just feeling lost or unhappy. Reading through the insights you have recorded about yourself in Take Stock can be heartening and reaffirming. Sometimes you will find the answer you are looking for just by reminding yourself about your Life Philosophy and Life Drivers; or by being kinder to yourself when considering your past and how that has shaped you.

REVIEW YOUR LIFE MAP REGULARLY

Set a time to review your Life Map annually. When conducting your review:

1. Read through your Take Stock. Reflect on your self-analysis in Steps 1 and 2 to make sure it still reflects who you are now. Consider whether your personalised statements and drivers still ring true, or if they require alteration or refinement. Also review Step 3 and ensure your world analysis is current; if not, what has changed? Were those changes deliberate and positive, or has something outside of your control impacted your environment?

2. Go over your Life Map. Consider the past 12 months, and where you may have gone off track, and the reasons for that detour; was it a pleasant accident or short-notice opportunity, or has something bad happened that caused you to hit the brakes before reaching some of your goals, or to change them altogether? Or did it unfold as planned?

3. Review your obstacle planning from Step 5. Did you need to refer to your risk assessments or Divergent Points over the course of the past year? Are there Divergent Points or important goals or milestones

coming up in your future that you have not previously considered and need to develop?

4. Make the necessary updates to your Life Map and reflect on the path you have walked over the past year. Feel proud for what you have achieved, take time to grieve for what you may have lost, feel grateful for where you are and what you **do** have, and be optimistic about the coming year and the opportunities waiting for you.

'Step 7': The Black Swan event

When I was a Staff Cadet training at the Royal Military College, Duntroon, our tactics lessons and assignments were based on the 6 Step Individual Military Appreciation Process, from which this Life Map Process has been derived. When it came time to deliver our plans to instructors for assessment, there was a running joke regarding 'Step 7'. For students, Step 7 was the uncontrollable factor of which instructor you were allocated for your assessment and whether that individual would be a hard or easy marker. Step 7 was something you had no control over; the same plan briefed to one instructor could win you top marks, but if briefed to someone else could earn barely a pass. In the high pressure and competitive world of military college, a bad mark could derail your progression. As any student knows, this problem is not restricted to the military; many of us have felt unfairly treated by a bad mark at school, or have chosen our university lecturers based on who has the reputation of being more lenient.

I want to talk about Step 7 here as a 'wild card' event. In Step 5 we assessed possible future events and devised options so that we are better prepared to deal with obstacles, or mitigate

Step 6: Take Command

their occurrence. However, the wild card or 'Black Swan' event is something so unanticipated that you are unlikely to have prepared for (or against).

I like the term 'Black Swan' to describe a wild card event. The term was coined to symbolise an impossibility: there is no such thing as a black swan in Europe – all swans are white. However, native black swans are plentiful in Australia, where the white swan is not a native animal. That the term was used in one part of the world to describe the impossible, when in fact it is the norm somewhere else, shows the potential for fallacy in declaring something to be impossible. You never can tell when a Black Swan event might attempt to force the course of your life in a different direction.

Something that we were all faced with in 2020 and 2021 was the worldwide pandemic – COVID-19. In an unprecedented event, billions of people around the globe found themselves suddenly in lockdown, with international and internal domestic borders closed. Many people suffered, either directly from infection with the virus, or because of the impact the restrictions had on their freedoms, plans, finances and separation from family. It often felt like we were all living in a Hollywood blockbuster movie. In many ways an event like this was not completely unexpected; the risk had been forewarned over decades by many scientists, politicians, health advocates and documentary and fiction film creators. Nonetheless, the event itself still took the world by surprise and rocked our foundations. In such an event, just about all plans come to a grinding halt; for some, the impacts could be far reaching. Just as '9/11' altered forever the processes of and restrictions to air travel, so too the impacts of COVID-19 have changed major aspects of our lives moving forward.

A Black Swan event could be more intimately personal – the death of a loved one, a traumatic accident, being diagnosed with a terminal illness – something out of the blue that irrevocably alters your life forever after. A Life Map can fall over completely in these circumstances. But I sincerely believe if you have taken the time to do Step 1 and 2, such that you now know yourself and your drivers, you can deal with anything life throws at you. At the end of the day, this is the one life you are guaranteed to have; you owe it to yourself to live it the best way you can. The way that will bring you the most happiness and fulfilment, regardless of your circumstances.

Step 6 Summary

You are now ready to Take Command! This step is really about having the confidence in yourself to take what you have put into your Life Map and turn it into reality. Reminding yourself of what is most important, reviewing and updating your Life Map as you move through your life and doing your best to prepare for curveballs and adapt to Black Swan events. While there is no 'one size fits all' approach to life planning, goal setting and contingency planning; the activities you have completed throughout this book can support your journey to take ownership and live your best life.

STEP 6 OUTCOMES
ACTIVITY 20: LIVE WITH YOUR LIFE MAP TO GUIDE YOU
ACTIVITY 21: REVIEW YOUR LIFE MAP REGULARLY

CHAPTER 9
CONCLUSION

> *A journey of a thousand miles must begin with a single step.*
> —Lao Tzu

YOU HAVE NOW stepped through a tried and tested military process modified and adapted into a life planning method. You may have learnt more about yourself, you may have learnt some new tools and techniques, and hopefully you have developed a plan that can serve as a guide as you move through your life – a Life Map that will help you stay true to yourself and the way you want to live your life with the people you choose to have with you on the way.

In following the Take Command Life Planning process, you have developed greater awareness of yourself and your life. You can look beyond little daily stressors and appreciate the bigger picture of where your life is heading. By taking the time to gain an enhanced understanding of yourself, you can be confident that you are now working towards creating the life

you want, not the life you think you are supposed to want. This can give you the strength to sacrifice today to work towards a goal, or the overall vision you have of the way you want your life to be. You also have the tools to implement, and have the motivation to sustain, those daily practices that will get you from where you are to where you want to be.

Life is a journey; while it is great to have a plan, if we rewind all the way back to Step 1, you'll remember the quote by Winston Churchill, *plans are of little importance, but planning is essential.* If you know yourself, know what is important to you, and have done the planning needed to create a Life Map, you have the tools you need to readjust when something happens that derails your plan. Being able to do this will give you a sense of control when life feels out of control, and lets you tackle adversity with confidence, as you have a way to work through the hardship.

It is time to Take Command and be in control of the direction your life is heading, to have each day filled with what you have identified will give you purpose and bring you happiness. Stop running for that blue ribbon if that is not what you actually want; join me in charting your own course and attaining your very own pink ribbon.

APPENDICES

Appendix 1

Rosenberg Self-Esteem Scale

Instructions

Below is a list of statements dealing with your general feelings about yourself. Please indicate how strongly you agree or disagree with each statement.

1. I feel that I'm a person of worth, at least on an equal plane with others

    a. Strongly Agree (3)

    b. Agree (2)

    c. Disagree (1)

    d. Strongly Disagree (0)

2. I feel that I have a number of good qualities.

    a. Strongly Agree (3)

    b. Agree (2)

    c. Disagree (1)

    d. Strongly Disagree (0)

3. All in all, I am inclined to feel that I am a failure.

    a. Strongly Agree (0)

    b. Agree (1)

    c. Disagree (2)

    d. Strongly Disagree (3)

4. I am able to do things as well as most other people.

    a. Strongly Agree

    b. Agree

    c. Disagree

    d. Strongly Disagree

    a. Strongly Agree (3)

    b. Agree (2)

    c. Disagree (1)

    d. Strongly Disagree (0)

5. I feel I do not have much to be proud of.

   a. Strongly Agree (0)

   b. Agree (1)

   c. Disagree (2)

   d. Strongly Disagree (3)

6. I take a positive attitude toward myself.

   a. Strongly Agree (3)

   b. Agree (2)

   c. Disagree (1)

   d. Strongly Disagree (0)

7. On the whole, I am satisfied with myself.

   a. Strongly Agree (3)

   b. Agree (2)

   c. Disagree (1)

   d. Strongly Disagree (0)

8. I wish I could have more respect for myself.

   a. Strongly Agree (0)

   b. Agree (1)

   c. Disagree (2)

   d. Strongly Disagree (3)

9. I certainly feel useless at times.

   a. Strongly Agree (0)

   b. Agree (1)

   c. Disagree (2)

   d. Strongly Disagree (3)

10. At times I think I am no good at all.

    a. Strongly Agree (0)

    b. Agree (1)

    c. Disagree (2)

    d. Strongly Disagree (3)

Scores are in brackets after each answer. Sum scores for all 10 items.

The scale ranges from 0–30, with 30 being the highest score possible. Higher scores indicate higher self-esteem.

My score:

So what?

Reference Rosenberg, M. (1965). Society and the adolescent self-image. Princeton, NJ: Princeton University Press.

Appendix 2

Generalised Self-Efficacy Scale

This questionnaire is a guide to assess your level of self-efficacy.

1. I can always manage to solve difficult problems if I try hard enough.

    a. not at all true (1)

    b. hardly true (2)

    c. moderately true (3)

    d. exactly true (4).

2. If someone opposes me, I can find the means and ways to get what I want.

    a. not at all true (1)

    b. hardly true (2)

    c. moderately true (3)

    d. exactly true (4).

3. I am certain that I can accomplish my goals.

    a. not at all true (1)

    b. hardly true (2)

    c. moderately true (3)

    d. exactly true (4).

4. I am confident that I could deal efficiently with unexpected events.

    a. not at all true (1)

    b. hardly true (2)

    c. moderately true (3)

    d. exactly true (4).

5. Thanks to my resourcefulness, I can handle unforeseen situations.

    a. not at all true (1)

    b. hardly true (2)

    c. moderately true (3)

    d. exactly true (4).

6. I can solve most problems if I invest the necessary effort.

    a. not at all true (1)

    b. hardly true (2)

    c. moderately true (3)

    d. exactly true (4).

7. I can remain calm when facing difficulties because I can rely on my coping abilities.

    a. not at all true (1)

    b. hardly true (2)

    c. moderately true (3)

    d. exactly true (4).

3. When I am confronted with a problem, I can find several solutions.

    a. not at all true (1)

    b. hardly true (2)

    c. moderately true (3)

    d. exactly true (4).

4. If I am in trouble, I can think of a good solution.

    a. not at all true (1)

    b. hardly true (2)

    c. moderately true (3)

    d. exactly true (4).

5. I can handle whatever comes my way.

    a. not at all true (1)

    b. hardly true (2)

    c. moderately true (3)

    d. exactly true (4).

Scores are in brackets after each answer. Sum scores for all 10 items.

Higher scores indicate higher self-efficacy on a scale of 10–40. The international average is 29.5.

My score:

So what?

Reference: Schwarzer, R., & Jerusalem, M. (1995). Generalized Self-Efficacy scale. In J. Weinman, S. Wright, & M. Johnston, Measures in health psychology: A user's portfolio. Causal and control beliefs (pp. 35 - 37). Windsor, England: NFER-NELSON.

Appendix 3

Life Map – Phase 0 Template

These templates can also be found at TakeCommandLifePlanning.com

Phase 0a.	Year – Year
Age	
Summary	<ul><li></li><li></li><li></li><li></li><li></li></ul>
Memories	<ul><li></li><li></li></ul>

Phase 0b.	Year – Year
Age	
Summary	<ul><li></li><li></li></ul>
Memories	<ul><li></li><li></li></ul>

Appendix 4

Life Map Template

Phase 1a.	Title (Year)	Priority Driver
January	• • •	
February	• • •	
March	• • •	
April	• • •	
May	• • •	
June	• • •	
July - September	• • •	
October – December	• • •	

Take Command!

Phase 1b	Title (Year)	Priority Driver
January to June	<ul><li></li><li></li><li></li></ul>	
July to December	<ul><li></li><li></li><li></li></ul>	

Phase 2	Title (Year - Year)	Priority Driver
Year	<ul><li></li><li></li></ul>	
Year	<ul><li></li><li></li></ul>	

Phase 3	Title (Year - Year)	Priority Driver
Year - Year	<ul><li></li><li></li></ul>	•

Appendix 5

Risk Assessment Template

GOAL / MILESTONE / EVENT:		
Risks	What could happen?	Treatment Options

Appendix 6

Divergent Point Templates

Divergent Point:		
Path A	Path B	Path C

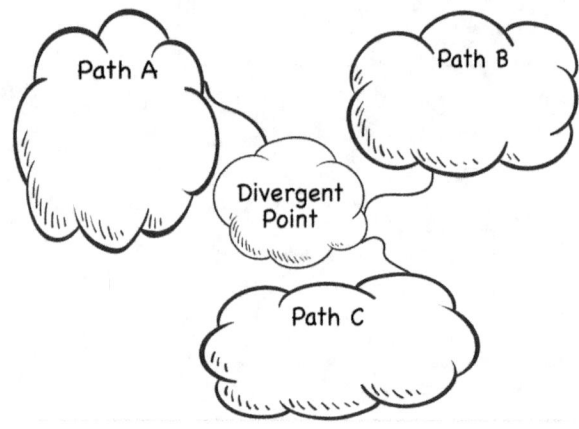

REFERENCE MATERIAL

Bandura, A., Ross, D., Ross, S.A., & Webb, D. (Ed). (2013). *Psychology Classics All Psychology Students Should Read: The Bobo Doll Experiment.* Createspace Independent Publishing.

Driskell, J. E., Copper, C., & Moran, A. (1994). Does mental practice enhance performance? *Journal of Applied Psychology*, 79(4), 481.

Gazzaniga, M.S., Ivry, R.B., Mangun, G.R. (2014). *Cognitive Neuroscience: The Biology of the Mind,* (4th ed). W.W. Norton & Company.

Higgins, E.T. (1987). Self-discrepancy: a theory relating self and affect. *Psychological review*, 94(3), 319–340.

Hogg, M., & Vaughan, G. (2014). *Social Psychology* (7th ed). Pearson.

Maltby, J., Day, L., & Macaskill, A. (2017). *Personality, Individual Differences and Intelligence,* (4th ed). Pearson Education Limited.

McCrae, R., & Costa, P.T. (1987). Validation of the five-factor model of personality across instruments and observers. *Journal of personality and social psychology, 52*(1), 81–90.

Passer, M.W., & Smith, R.E. (2013). *Psychology: The Science of Mind and Behaviour,* (Australian ed). McGraw-Hill, Australia.

Steiner, K.L., Pillemer, D.B., & Thomsen, D.K. (2019). Writing About Life Story Chapters Increases Self-esteem: Three Experimental Studies. *Journal of Personality, 87*(5), 962–980.

Tufvesson, A. (2020). Health and wellbeing: Health: The downsides of positivity. *LSJ: Law Society of NSW Journal,* (73), 52–53.

Ulrich, R.S., Zimring, C., Joseph, A., & Choudhary, R. (2004). The role of the physical environment in the hospital of the 21st century. *The Center for Health Design.*

Ulrich, R.S., Zimring, C., Zhu, X., DuBose, J., Seo, H. B., Choi, Y.S., Quan, X., & Joseph, A. (2008). A review of the research literature on evidence-based healthcare design. *HERD, 1*(3), 61–125.

ACKNOWLEDGEMENTS

Over the years, the knowledge and experience I have gained in the Australian Army has sharpened my natural interest in planning and organisation. I have instinctively incorporated methods and tools I have learnt on military courses, exercises and operations into the way I plan and problem solve in my own life. So I must first acknowledge the many instructors, colleagues and commanders, from the Australian Defence Force and from Defence Force personnel I have worked with from around the world, who have shared their own knowledge and skills with me.

My thanks also go to the team at Author Academy Elite for their guidance and support on my publishing journey. And thanks to Michael Kuter, my editor, whose insight and patience was instrumental in getting this book ready for publication.

Acknowledgements

I prevailed upon family and friends to critique the many versions of my manuscript in the development of this book, and the finished product is a testament to you all. In particular, I must thank Karina, Paul, Sean, Helen, and Oliver; the ideas you inspired, and your constructive feedback was invaluable.

Finally, many thanks to my parents, Ruth and Peter, for your constant support. And to my son Bryson, my greatest inspiration.

www.ingramcontent.com/pod-product-compliance
Lightning Source LLC
LaVergne TN
LVHW011835060526
838200LV00053B/4045